ABOUT PREZI

One of the greatest innovations in education was the blackboard. For the first time in history, teachers could present their lessons visually and engage students to participate in the conversation. The whiteboard has done the same for business—helping us to explore and share ideas more effectively.

Prezi is a virtual whiteboard that transforms presentations from monologues into conversations: enabling people to see, understand, and remember ideas.

Seeing is believing and a picture can tell a thousand words, but a picture doesn't tell an entire story. A visual story has a flow and narrative, where images and words work together to present an idea or lesson. Use Prezi's open canvas to construct a story arc, where visual context leads the viewer on a path of discovery.

To understand complexity, one must zoom out to see the big picture and in to see the details. Prezi's 3-dimensional canvas is a virtual space where you can delve deeper and pan wider to broaden the conversation.

People remember spaces and stories. Prezi's use of spatial metaphor helps your audience remember your content better. Each prezi is a place where you can use spatial metaphor to engage your audience's memory.

MAKE AN IMPACT

THE STEP BY STEP GUIDE TO MASTERING PREZI

KYLE MACRAE

Published by Blasted Heath

ISBN-13: 978-1-908688-52-1

CONTENTS

1 INTRODUCTION

Back in 2008, I founded Blether Media, a social media marketing agency. I was running a lot of training courses and delivering a lot of presentations back then, and they were all developed with PowerPoint. You know how it goes. You fire up your slide deck with a generic template, and glance at your speaker notes and hope they'll help, then the first bullet point appears on screen... and you can sense, perhaps even hear, a suppressed sigh from the audience as they prepare once again for Death by PowerPoint. Ugh.

Then one day something interesting happened. I saw a presenter using Prezi (badly, as it happens) and decided to give this interesting new tool a try myself. Now, you know when you use an iPad for the first time and think: "Ah, so *this* is how it should be!" Prezi was like that for me. It still is.

Prezi offers an alternative way to design and present. Whether it's an internal presentation, a sales pitch, a training course, an external conference, or a platform for showcasing your business, Prezi prises you free from the forced linearity of slides – and make you tell a story. It gives you the power to deliver a stunning presentation that makes an impact, sticks in the memory and gets people talking. And it gives you a massive competitive advantage over the PowerPoint-bound competition.

About this book

This book is a distilled version of my hands-on Prezi training course which I've delivered to company teams and individuals over the past four years. In these pages, I have deliberately avoided fluffy stuff about design theory, cinematography, 'ideation', the theoretical benefits of non-linearity... and focussed instead on the how-to mechanics. I know where people tend to get stuck with Prezi, so I've addressed all of those areas.

What I *don't* know is whether you have any experience with Prezi, so I'm going to assume nothing more than you've seen it in action and *may* have dabbled. If you haven't seen it, get yourself along to prezi.com/explore and have a play with some prezis.

Just one thing. You can read this book in bed or on the train if you like but you'll achieve a whole lot more if you follow it step-by-step and page-by-page while actually using Prezi. That's how I've written it: to be used from start to finish as a hands-on manual while you work. Go at your own pace but don't skip anything. By the end, which is only 80-odd pages away, you'll be using Prezi confidently and competently.

And you know what? I'd love to see the prezis that you go on to create. See p90 for my contact details – and also for an offer of support.

2 SIGNING UP

Prezi operate a 'freemium' model, which means you can use it for free if you're content to put up with some inconveniences or pay if you want the full product with every feature. You even have a choice over how much to pay depending upon which features you need.

With the free account, you can only create prezis online (more of which in a moment) and you can't make your prezis private. This makes it unsuitable for developing, say, an internal presentation of your 'how we're going to rule the world' financial forecasts, because the world could potentially find that presentation on the web. If you have five minutes, try searching for company names on **prezi.com/explore** and see what you can discover that, er, probably shouldn't be public. Free prezis are also cobbled with a Prezi logo in the bottom corner.

If you upgrade from free to an ENJOY account ($59 annually), you can work ditch the Prezi logo for your own and you can make your prezis private. You still can't work offline, however. Move up to a PRO account ($159 annually) and you do get the benefits of an offline editor.

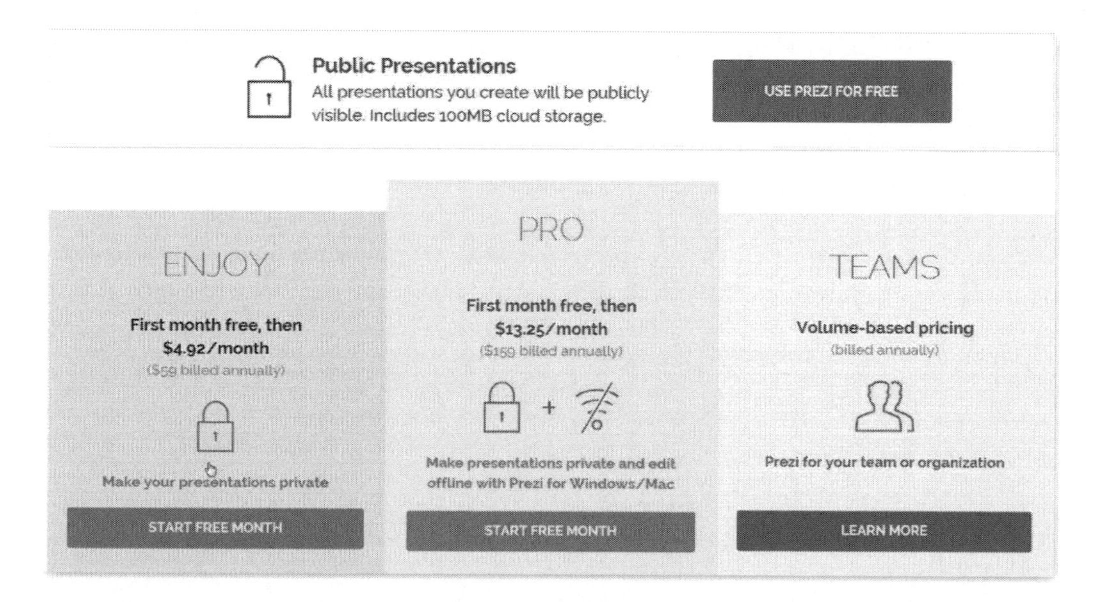

So is it worth the extra expense? Probably. Working online means having to design prezis in your browser, which is fine so long as you have a good internet connection and hopeless if you don't. The good news is that you can use the offline editor for a month when you sign up for a free trial of an ENJOY account. If you find that you can't live without it, upgrade to a PRO account and you can work offline forever. If you're happy working with your browser, stick with ENJOY.

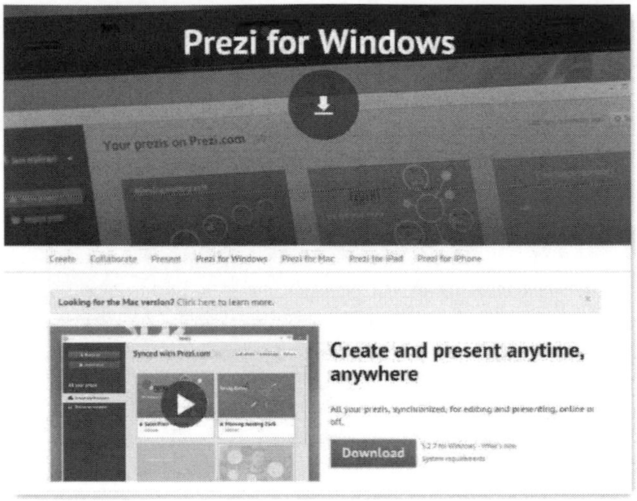

And if Prezi drives you nuts and you just can't stand the damned thing, cancel your account within 30 days and you won't be charged. It's true to say that most of the people I've trained in Prezi had already given it a go before booking me and had got stuck or frustrated or both. Perhaps you're the same. Who can blame you? Prezi is not the most intuitive software in the world – although it is way better than it used to be.

I'm going to prevent such frustration from hampering your enjoyment of Prezi. So grab yourself a trial ENJOY (or PRO) account from **prezi.com** and download Prezi for Windows.

Couple of quick notes:

- I'm working with a PC, not a Mac. But the differences are minimal and inconsequential.
- I'm adopting Prezi's convention for calling a presentation created with Prezi a prezi (lower case).
- Prezi is ever-evolving. As I write this, I'm using version 5.2.7 of Prezi for Windows, the desktop application. I'll keep this book updated as best I can but you may find that things aren't exactly where I say they are. Hopefully they won't be far away. Unless, that is, Prezi undertakes another massive overhaul and changes everything, in which case I'll write a completely new edition.
- To get highly irregular updates from me when things *do* change in Prezi, sign up for my newsletter on **blethermedia.com**

3 DIVING IN – YOUR FIRST PREZI

Prezi is a cloud-based service. Every prezi you create 'lives' in your Prezi account and can be accessed, edited and downloaded from any browser on any internet-connected computer (or iPad). This is highly convenient. However, you can also create prezis offline using a desktop application called Prezi for Windows (or Mac). To keep everything together, you need to synchronise your offline prezis with your online account.

Once upon a not so long ago, you did this by manually uploading offline prezis to your account in the Prezi cloud. It was a fraught, clunky process that often failed, at least in my experience. Prezi has now fixed this by making it easy to sync prezis with the cloud directly from within the Prezi for Windows application. Trouble is, Prezi's implementation of this feature is a little confusing, so let's get things clear right from the outset.

STEP 1

Fire up Prezi for Windows and note the left-hand sidebar. There are two categories: SYNCED WITH PREZI.COM and ONLY ON MY COMPUTER. Within these categories, you can see all your synced prezis and all your local prezis.

Local prezis exist only on your computer and can not be seen or edited from your prezi.com account. Synced prezis can be accessed and edited either from your computer or from your prezi.com account.

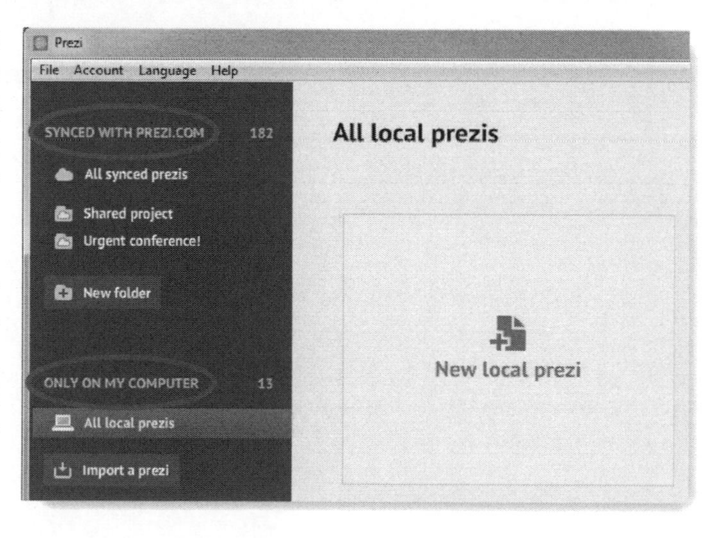

STEP 2

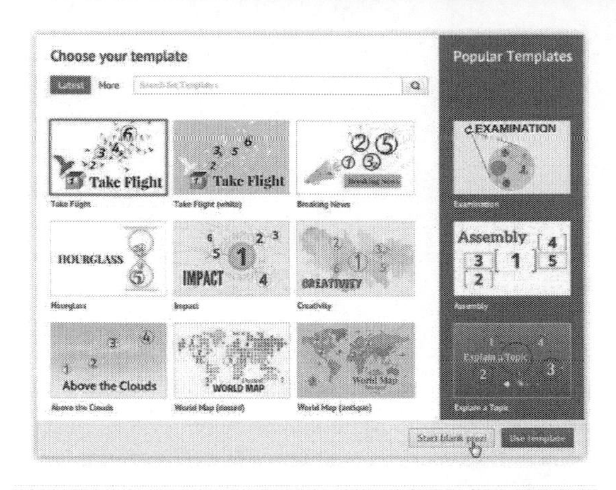

Select **All local prezis** and click **New local prezi**. This will launch a new window that invites you to select a template or start a blank prezi. You might want to browse through the templates – some are rather nice; others are clichéd and overused – but once you've had a look ignore them all and start a new, blank prezi instead.

STEP 3

You'll now see three things: a blue circle, two prompts to add text, and a big white expanse of nothingness, called the Prezi canvas. Think of it as a really big sheet of paper. The circle is technically a Prezi frame. Frames are a central element in Prezi, as we shall discover in detail.

This is your first chance to work with objects on the Prezi canvas. Click the larger, bolder text and type something (anything you like). Then repeat this for the second line of text. Simple, isn't it?

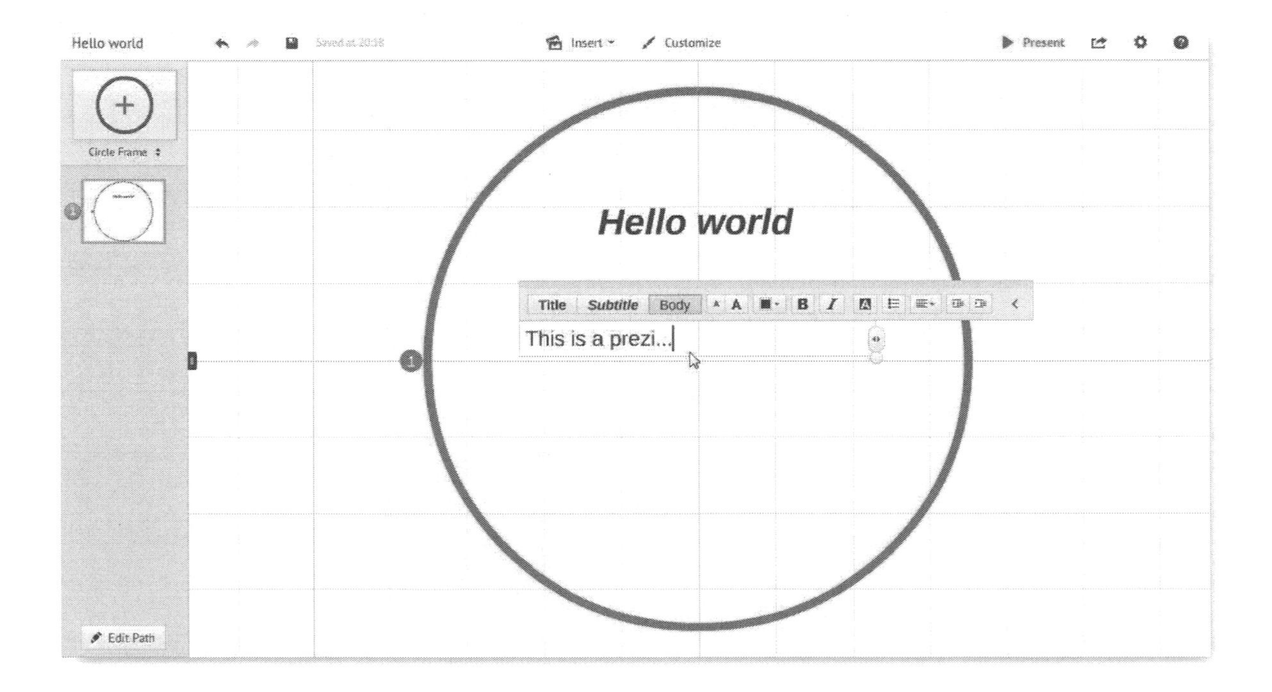

STEP 4

When you have two lines of text in place, carefully click the circumference of the blue circle frame. You should see a square box appear, which indicates that you have *selected* the frame. In the menu at the top, click **Delete**. The circle and its contents will disappear, leaving only the blank canvas.

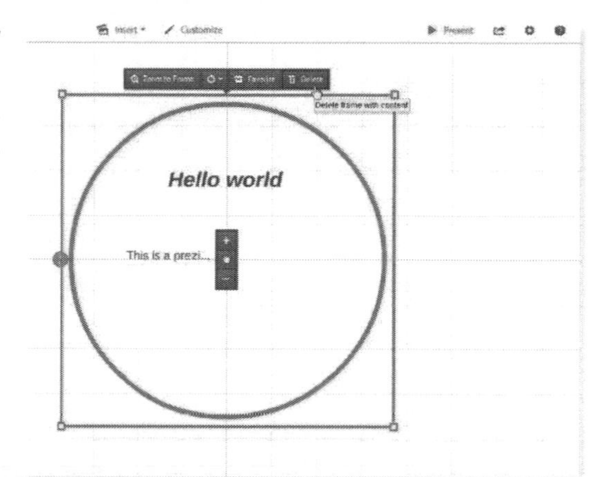

Although you only selected the circle frame, frames 'group' contents, which means whatever you do to a frame affects whatever's inside it. By deleting this frame, you deleted the text as well.

STEP 5

Anywhere on the blank canvas, click once. Up pops a text box and a menu that looks a little like what you'd see in a word processor. It includes three font choices: **Title**, **Subtitle** and **Body**. Click the **Title** option and type something.

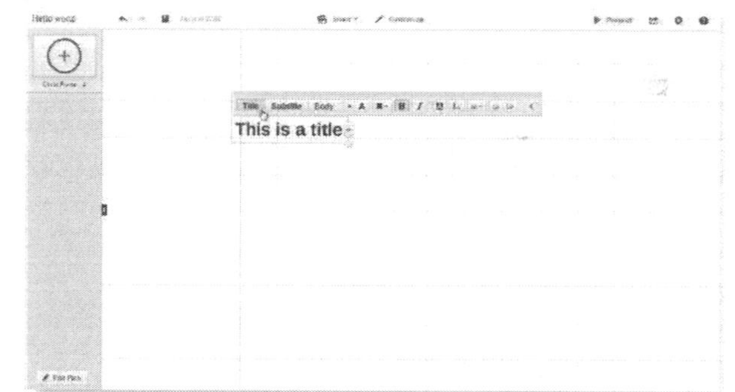

Now, while you may think you've just added a line of text, and while it *looks* like a line of text, as far as Prezi is concerned words on the canvas are no different to a photograph or a diagram. Everything is an *object*.

STEP 6

Click somewhere nearby on the canvas and add another line of text, this time selecting the **Subtitle** option. Then repeat once more and add some **Body** text. You'll end up with three separate objects on the canvas.

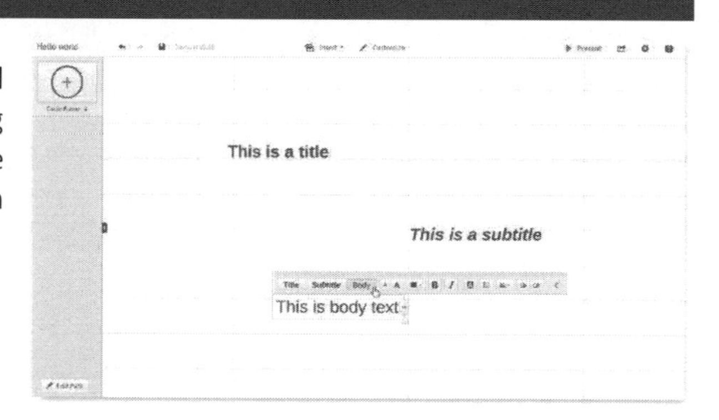

STEP 7

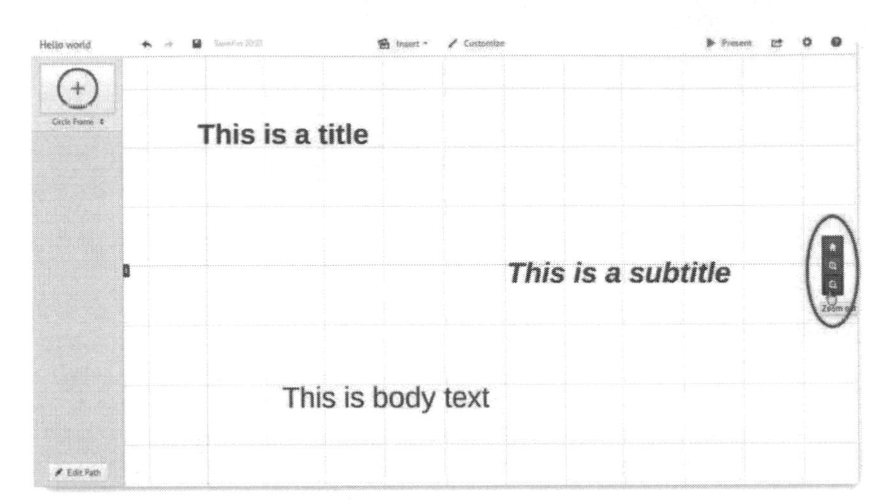

Now familiarise yourself with the canvas itself and how you get around. If you click on the canvas and don't let go of the mouse button, you can drag the canvas left, right, up and down. Try dragging the canvas so that your text objects slide right out of the window, and then drag the canvas in the opposite direction to bring them back into view again. If you have a mouse with a wheel (which is very helpful for working with Prezi), try scrolling the wheel to make the text objects larger and smaller. If you don't have a wheel mouse, hover over to the right-hand side of the canvas and use the plus and minus magnifying glass buttons to change scale. There's also a **Home** button there (it looks like a house) that will bring your three text objects back into view when you lose them on the near-infinite canvas.

Now, despite appearances, you haven't been making the objects larger and smaller at all. Rather, you have been zooming in and out of the canvas. Imagine a camera looking down on the canvas from above. When you use the mouse wheel or plus button to make things bigger, you're actually zooming in on the canvas; and when you use the minus button, you're zooming out. The objects on the canvas don't change size at all; it's just your view of them that's changing.

This zooming is a central feature in Prezi and you should practise now until you're comfortable zooming in and out of the canvas and dragging it in different directions.

STEP 8

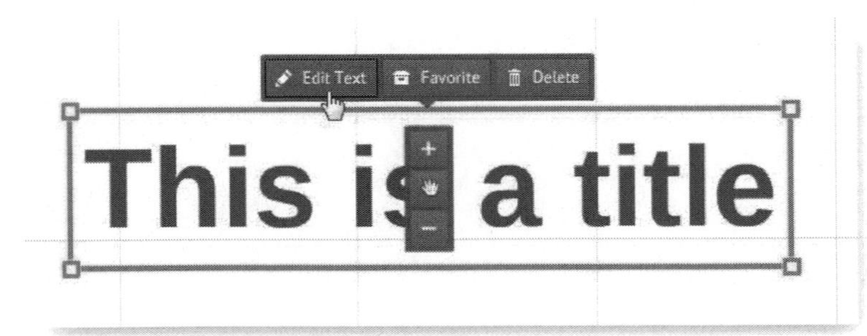

Click on one of your text objects. Just as in Step 4 above, you'll see a blue selectio box appear around the words to signify that the object has been selected. Again, you'll see a **Delete** button. However, because this is a text object, there's a new button in the menu: **Edit Text**. Click this now to open the text box and to access the text options.

STEP 9

Try adding an extra word or two until your text splits into two lines, then note the handle on the right-hand side of the text box. You can drag this left and right to contract or expand the width of the text box, and the text will flow accordingly.

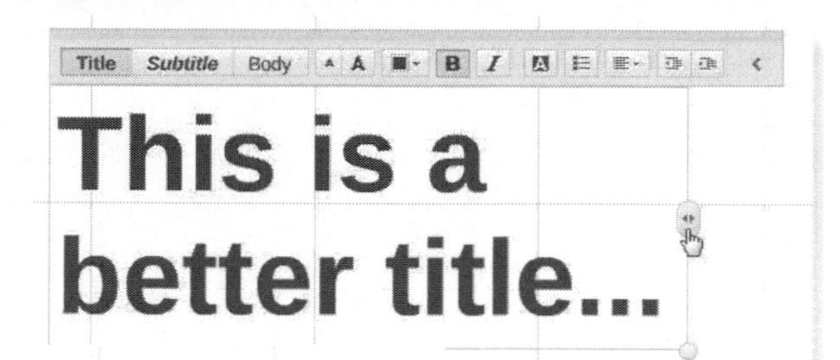

STEP 10

Other options in the menu include adding shading behind text, using a bold or italics style, and changing text colour. You can change all text at once by highlighting everything or highlight just a single word to change its colour in isolation. If you want to use a particular text colour consistently for your **Title**, **Subtitle** or **Body** text, you can set this in the Theme Wizard (see p28).

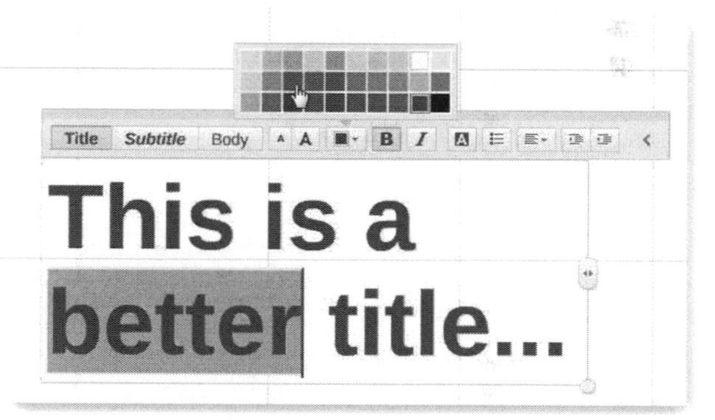

You can also left-align, right-align and justify text, and even add ironic PowerPoint-style bullets.

STEP 11

The most valuable lesson in this book: hit the **Save** button! In fact, hit it frequently. Prezi for Windows is dreadfully prone to freezing and crashing on a PC and can, despite an autosave feature, lose recent edits. So hit **Save** – or use the **Ctrl + S** keystroke combination – to save your prezis every couple of minutes as you go along. When you've saved your current prezi, close it by clicking the cross in the top right-hand corner of the window. Your Prezi for Windows dashboard should still be open and your new prezi should appear as a thumbnail in the **All local prezis** section.

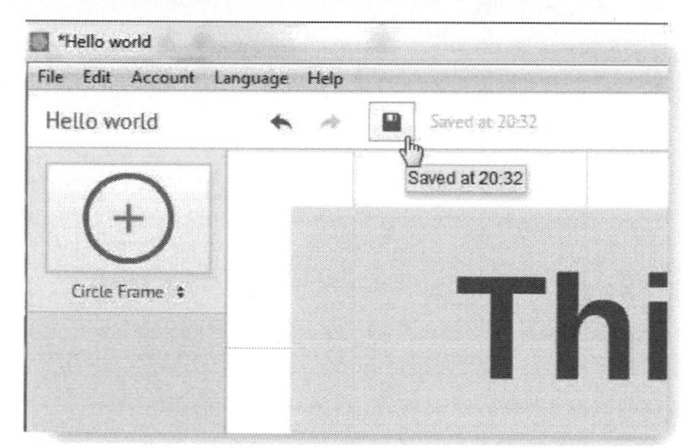

STEP 12

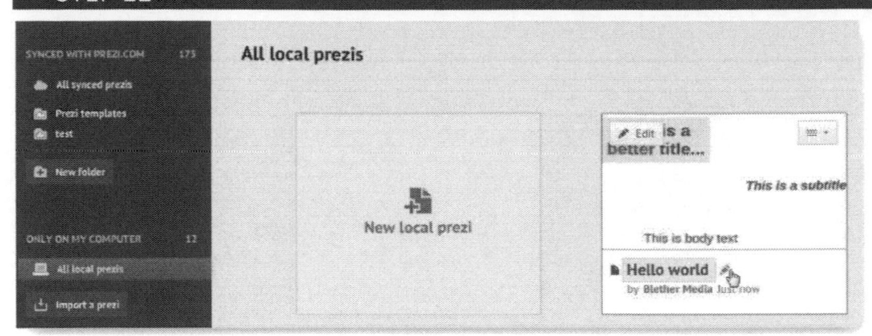

Two things to do now. First, click the little pen symbol next to your prezi's title and give it a more useful name.

Secondly, click the menu button in the top-right corner of the thumbnail. Here you'll see an option to sync this prezi with your Prezi account, so click this. Just to be clear about syncing again:

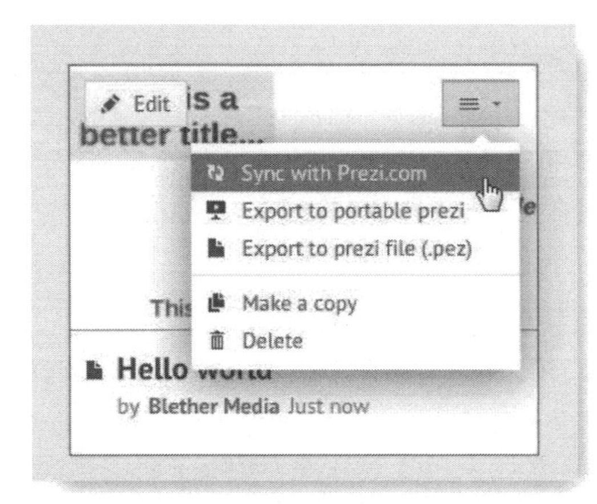

- You've just created a local prezi (Step 2). For now, this prezi only exists on your computer.

- When you click **Sync with Prezi.com**, a copy of your prezi will be uploaded to your Prezi account. You'll now be able to see and edit it online from anywhere simply by logging into your Prezi account at prezi.com.

- At the same time, in the Prezi for Windows application your prezi will move from the **All local prezis** section to the **All synced prezis** section.

STEP 13

To reopen your prezi, hover over the thumbnail in **All synced prezis** and click the **Edit** button. This will launch the editing window and you can continue from where you left off (remembering to save, save, and save once again).

Note that if you click the thumbnail itself *rather* than the **Edit** button, your prezi will open in a player window that allows you to present but not edit. We'll be looking at Present mode later.

STEP 14

A couple of other notes before we crack on. When you work on the prezi.com website, any prezis that you create online are automatically synced with Prezi for Windows. That is, you don't have to manually initiate a sync as you do when you create new local prezis in Prezi for Windows (Step 12).

When you open Prezi for Windows for the first time after creating a new prezi online, you should see a thumbnail for that prezi in the **All synced prezis** section. If you don't, click the **Refresh** button to tell Prezi for Windows to go find the new prezi.

When the thumbnail appears in Prezi for Windows, you have to download it from your online account before you can open or edit it. Just hover over the greyed-out thumbnail and click **Download**. Once you've done this, any edits that you subsequently make to the prezi in Prezi for Windows will be automatically synced with your prezi.com account.

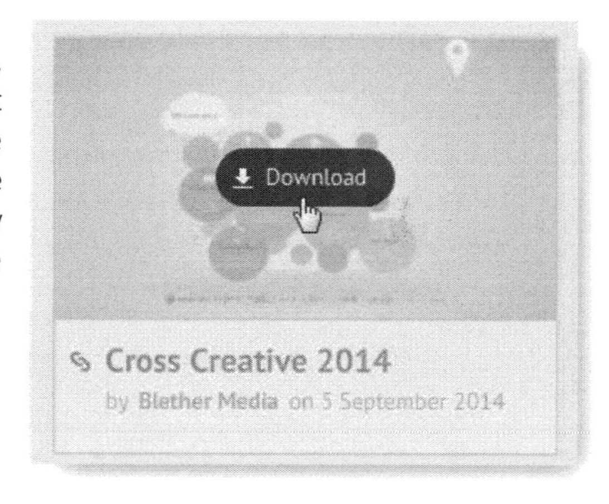

4 WORKING WITH OBJECTS ON THE CANVAS

So far, you've created a new prezi from scratch, added and edited some text, and synced it between Prezi for Windows and prezi.com. Not bad! Now let's spend some quality time working with objects on the canvas.

STEP 1

As before, start a new, blank prezi, delete the circle frame that appears by default, and add three text objects on the canvas using the **Title**, **Subtitle** and **Body** options.

Now select one of the text objects with a click and ensure that the blue selection box appears.

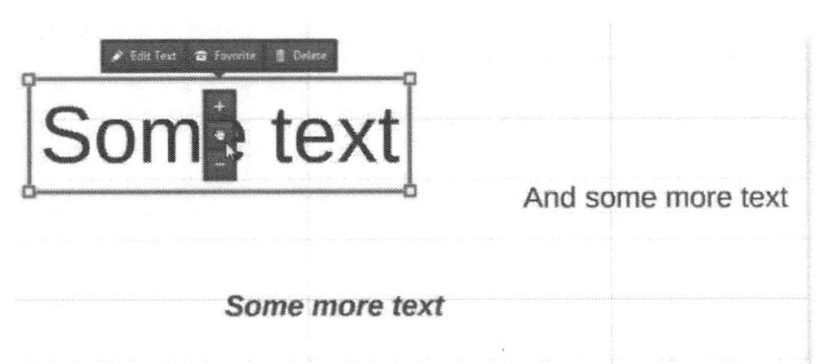

You've already seen the **Edit Text** and **Delete** buttons so this time note the three buttons in the middle of the object. This is the Transformation Tool. Sounds grand, doesn't it? Click and hold the middle button, which has a hand icon, and drag the object around the canvas. You'll find that you can reposition it anywhere you like.

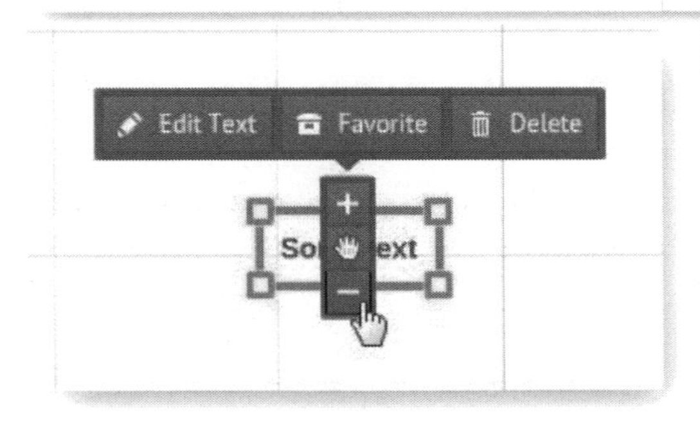

STEP 2

For its next trick, the Transformation Tool allows you to resize objects. Try clicking the plus and minus buttons. You can scale the text up and down from massive to virtually invisible.

STEP 3

The resize buttons scale an object in regular jumps. For finer control over scale, look for the little square handles in each corner of the selection box. Click and hold a handle and then drag in and out to scale the object at will.

STEP 4

To rotate an object, use the same corner handles. This time, however, hover over a handle until it grows a little circle extension. Click and hold this extension and you can drag the object through 360 degrees of rotation on the canvas.

STEP 5

Now, something may have occurred to you earlier when you were editing text for the first time. With all this talk of making text bigger and smaller, where exactly is the font size option? It wasn't in the text edit menu earlier (Steps 9-10 on p15).

This is because there's no such thing as absolute scale in Prezi. There's only relative scale. You can't make one line of text 12pt and another line 24pt; you can only make any line of text relatively bigger or smaller than any other line. How *much* larger or smaller is entirely your choice.

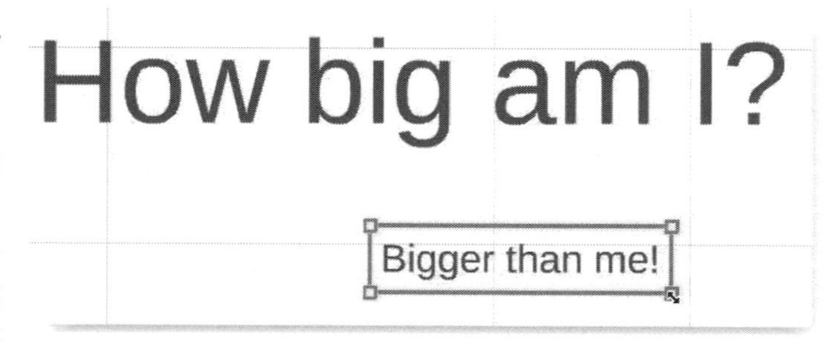

This apparent lack of precision and consistency leads to some confusion in Prezi. It's one of the areas where first-time users tend to get a bit baffled, particularly when they want to make two pieces of text the same size. Surely it's not *all* done by eye and guesswork?

STEP 6

Not quite. Use the Transformation Tool to drag one text object fairly close to another, as shown here. Then select one of the objects – in this case, the text that begins **And some** is selected – and carefully drag the corner handles. When a faint box appears around the *other* text object – **Some text**, in this example – you know that the objects are now the same size on the canvas. In effect, they have the same font size; it's just that putting an actual number on that size would be meaningless on the Prezi canvas where scale is relative.

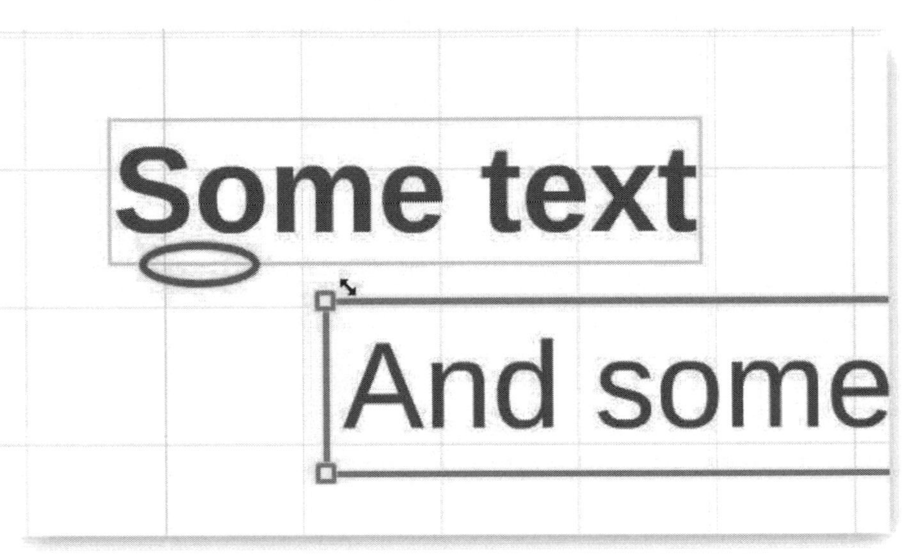

STEP 7

In a similar way, you can align objects vertically and horizontally on the canvas. Just drag them into close proximity and look for the dotted line that pops up when they're positioned on the same horizontal or vertical plane.

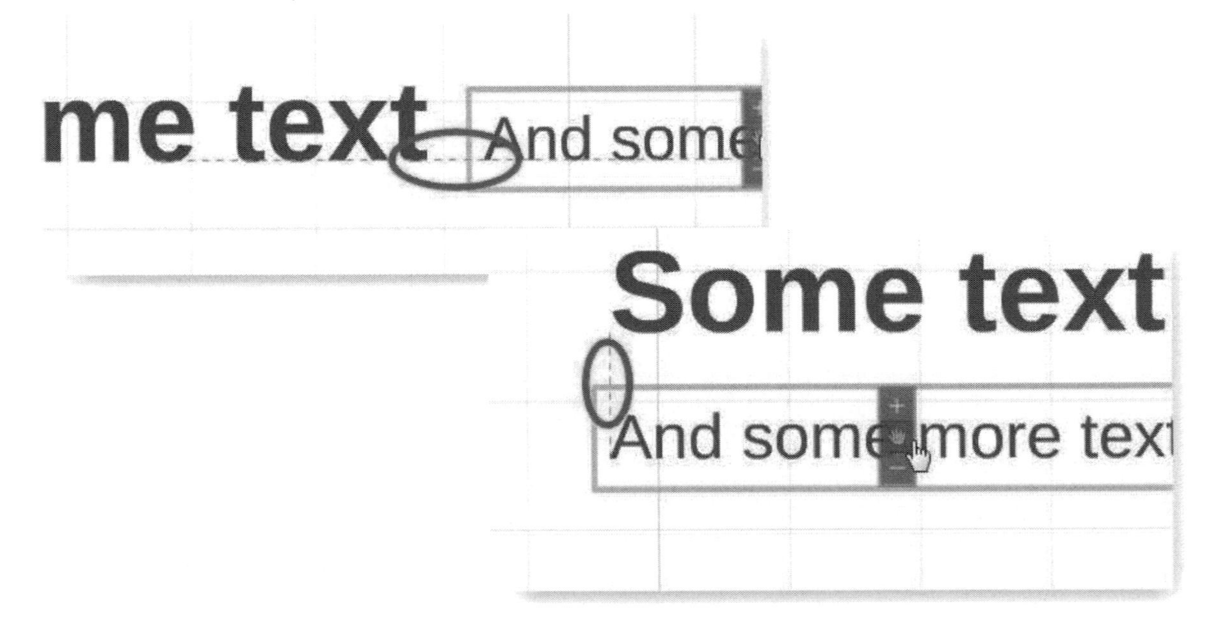

STEP 8

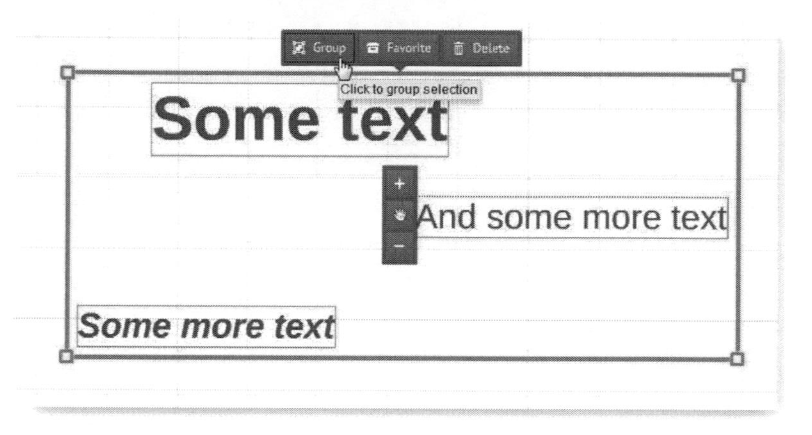

Sometimes it's useful to group objects. This allows you to move, scale, rotate, copy or delete two or more objects at the same time just as if they were a single object. To group objects, select the first object with a click. Now hold down the **Ctrl** key on your keyboard and select a second object. Continue holding the Ctrl key until you have selected each object that you want to group, and then release the key. You'll see a menu like this. Click **Group**. Now you can use the Transformation Tool to edit the entire group together.

Note that you can also group objects by holding down the **Shift** key and using your mouse to draw a selection box around them on the canvas. This has exactly the same effect. However, it's a bit fiddly and it doesn't work when you want to group two objects when there's a third object in the way. That's the case in this example where I want to group the two rotated objects but not the line of text between them.

You can ungroup objects at any point just by selecting any object that's in a group and clicking **Ungroup** in the popup menu.

STEP 9

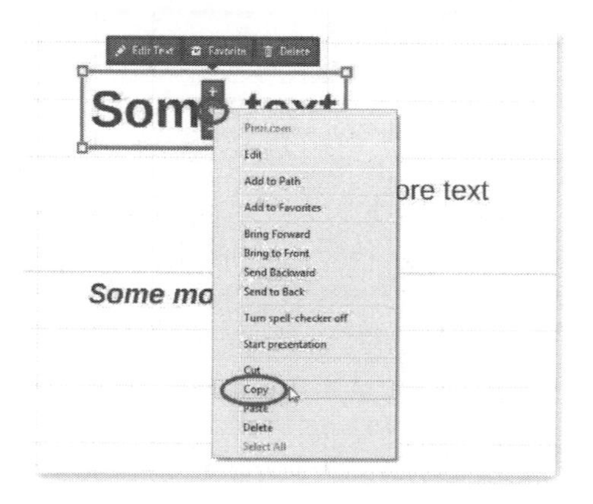

Often in a presentation, you'll want various content to be the same size. This might be true for text titles or captions. Rather than manually scaling new text each time, as in Step 6, you can simply copy and paste objects.

To copy, select an object on the canvas and either use the **Ctrl + C** key combination, or right-click the handle in the Transformation Tool and select **Copy** from the menu. Now right-click anywhere on the canvas and paste the object (or group) that you just copied. However...

STEP 10

There's a snag with copy and paste in prezi. If you zoom in or out of the canvas *between* copying and pasting, scale is affected. For instance, if you copy a text object from one part of the canvas and then zoom in or out before you paste it, the object may be pasted at a different scale to the original. That's a drag.

As an alternative, try duplication instead. Select a text object and use the **Ctrl + D** keystroke combination. This will generate a copy of the object and place it next to the original. The new content will also be pre-selected ready for manipulation. It will even be duplicated on exactly the same horizontal plane as the original (which is useful, as we'll see in action on p46). Now you can drag the new content anywhere you like on the canvas knowing that it's the same size as the original.

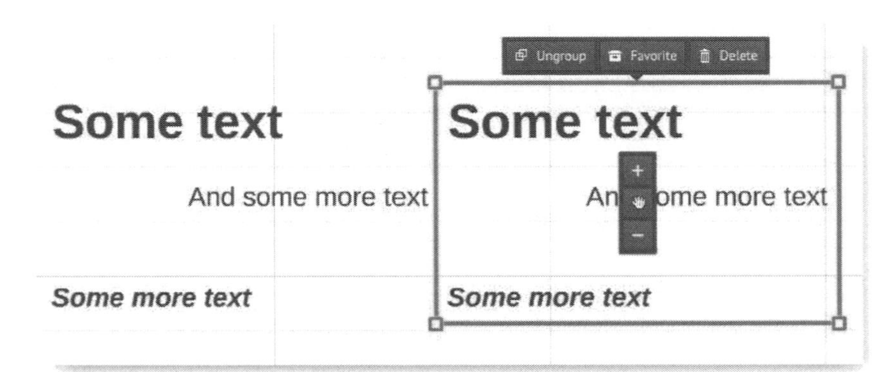

Duplication works with single objects and with grouped content. In this example, the three text objects on the left are grouped. This group was then selected and duplicated. The new content, shown with the selection box around it, appears alongside the original on the same horizontal plane.

STEP 11

When you come to design your own prezis, you'll learn the importance of scale for telling a visual story. Simply put, bigger things (including text) on the canvas *look* more important than smaller things, and you should always emphasise whatever's most important.

But you can also use scale within a single block of text, as shown here. Unfortunately, you can't resize a single word *within* a text object so to get this effect you need to use three text boxes. First, type **Think about**. Now duplicate it to make a second text object that's the same size. Edit the text in the new object to read **for emphasis** and drag it down and to the side. Now make a third text object, **SCALE**, and make it much bigger. Drag the three objects into place and then group them so they behave as a single object.

5 WORKING WITH IMAGES

Remember the first good prezi you ever saw? Chances are it had strong, dramatic, memorable imagery – literal or metaphorical – and very few words. Whether you use detailed images to illustrate a complex technical process, or a single visual metaphor (like the cover of this book), images bring your presentations to life. Use them widely, boldly and imaginatively. Here's what you need to know.

STEP 1

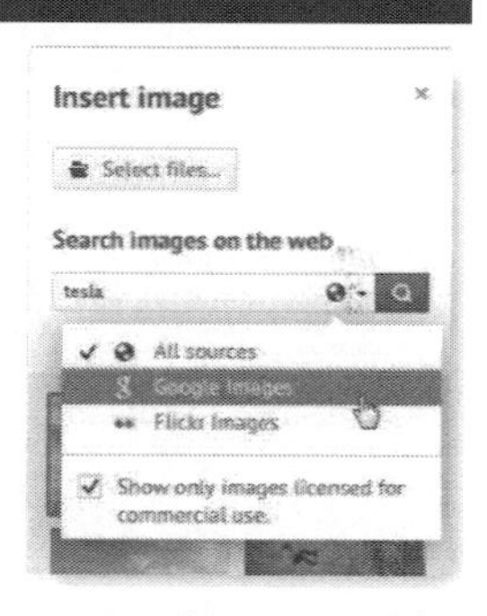

In any prezi, click the **Insert** button on the toolbar, followed by **Image**. You now have two choices: grab a picture from the web or use your own. Generally, you'll want to use your own images in your presentations, in which case use the **Select files** button to add what you need from your computer or network. However, for an internal, private presentation, you may well find what you need in Google Images or Flickr. If your presentation is going to be shown publicly – which would include embedding a prezi on your website – select the commercial licensing option. You might also want to consider stock image libraries like shutterstock.com and istockphoto.com.

STEP 2

If you're using the web option, search on a key term and drag images from the sidebar straight onto the canvas (or double-click them, which does the same thing).

STEP 3

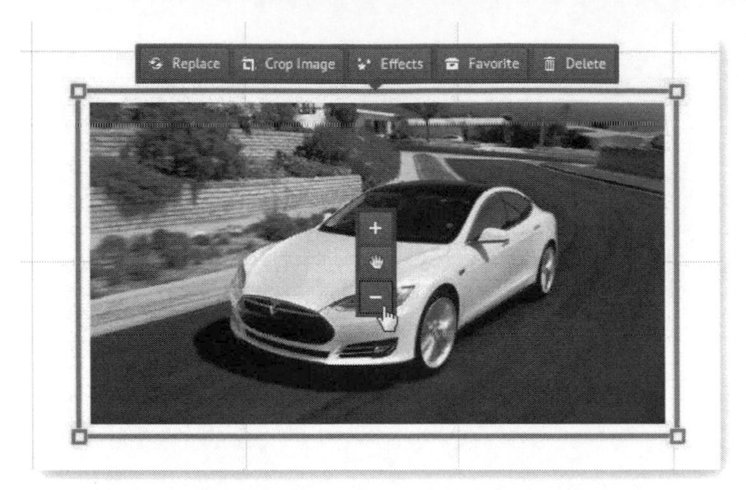

When you select an image on the canvas, the Transformation Tool lets you move, scale, rotate, copy/paste (or duplicate) and otherwise manipulate that image much like a text object. Remember, to Prezi one object on the canvas is much like any other. That said, there are some differences.

For example, the image menu includes a **Replace** option to swap one image for another. This is more useful than it sounds, as Prezi makes the new image the same size and shape as the original so it will fit with your design.

STEP 4

The **Crop Image** tool works a treat, letting you drag handles to remove areas of an image. The greyed-out sections disappear when you click away, leaving a neatly cropped picture. It's a nice touch that saves you having to work in a separate image-editing program like Photoshop.

STEP 5

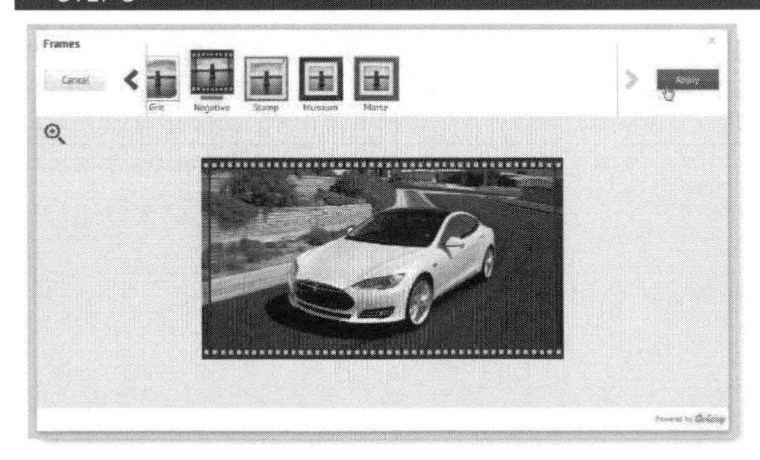

So too does the **Effects** menu. A host of options here help you change the colour and appearance of any image. Select a main menu item, such as **Frames**, and work through the options. Clicking **Apply** shows you a real-time preview of the effect. Click **Cancel** to return to the main menu or **Save** to apply your effect and return to the canvas.

STEP 6

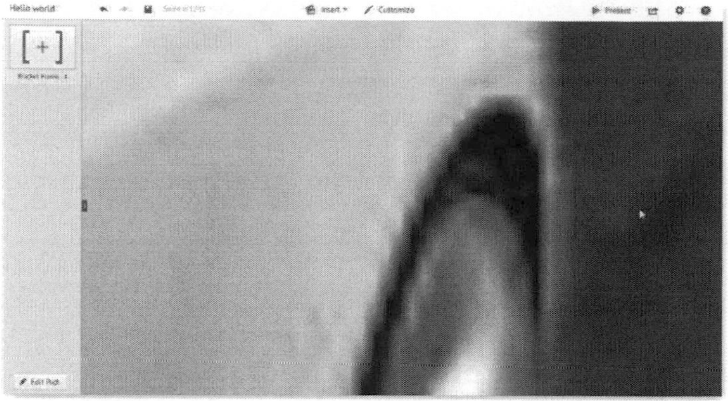

There are two types of image: raster (including JPEG, GIF and PNG file formats), and vector (including EPS, AI and PDF file formats). A raster image is displayed on screen by means of tiny dots, or pixels. This can be a problem because as you zoom in on the canvas the pixels may become visible. To minimise this, use high resolution raster images. High resolution means more pixels, which means less chance of seeing them as you zoom. This is particularly important when using images as backgrounds or showing them full screen.

Vector images do *not* pixelate and can be scaled without any loss of definition. We'll see some vector images in just a moment (Steps 9 -11 on p26-27).

STEP 7

Here's another image consideration: transparency. Prezi supports PNG files, a format that allows parts of an image to be rendered transparent. In this example, what you're looking at is an image comprised of text on a black background. The letters have been made transparent and the image saved as a PNG file. It has then been placed on top of a separate image of DNA, which shows through the transparent letters. This can be extremely effective. Unfortunately, Prezi itself doesn't help you make transparent PNG files so this is something that has to be done in an image editing program.

STEP 8

When you insert an image on the canvas, think of it as dropping a picture on a table. If you were to drop a second image in the same spot, it would lie on top of the first image. Add a third image and you'd be well on the way to building a stack. The Prezi canvas works in the same way. Put multiple images in the same space on the canvas and they get layered, with the most recent image always at the top.

Sometimes, you may want to change the order of the layers. In this example, the people picture overlaps the dog picture. To change this, select the bottom image and right-click the hand icon in the Transformation Tool. Now click **Bring Forward** to raise it by a single layer or **Bring to Front** to make it the topmost layer on the entire canvas.

STEP 9

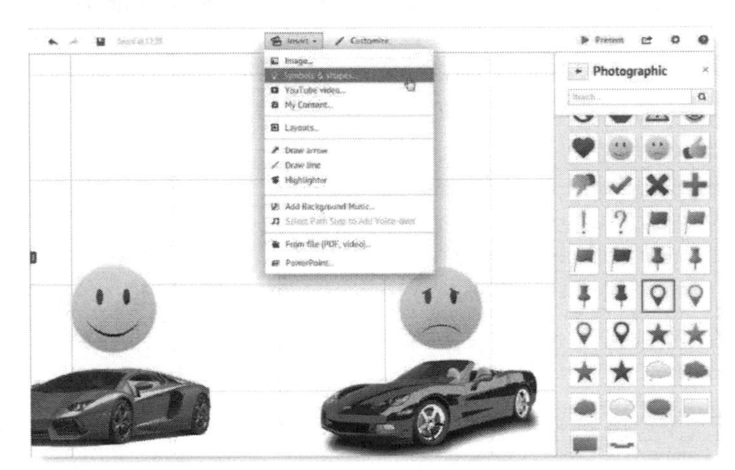

Prezi comes with a built-in collection of imagery, some of it reasonable and some of it awful. You'll find **Symbols & shapes** via the **Insert** menu. Have a browse through the collections and if you see something you like drag it onto the canvas from the sidebar. Everything here is vector-based to it can be scaled without any pixilation or loss of resolution.

Also in the **Insert** menu, you'll find some drawing options, including arrows and lines and a scribbly highlighter. Click any tool and draw shapes directly onto the canvas. When you draw an arrow or a line, you'll see a mini menu that allows you to change thickness and colour. However, a better way to set colours is through the Theme Wizard, as we'll see in the next chapter.

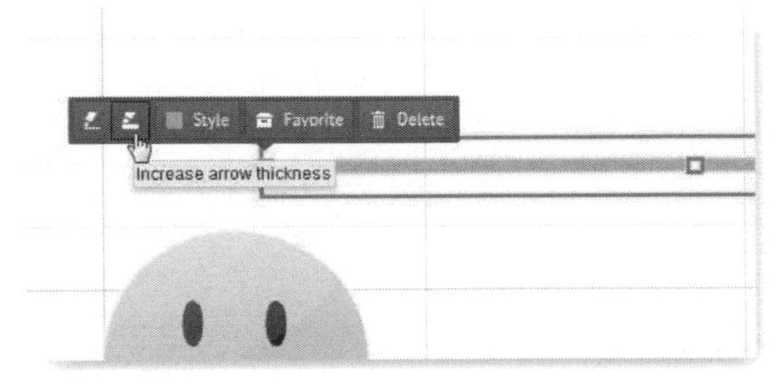

STEP 10

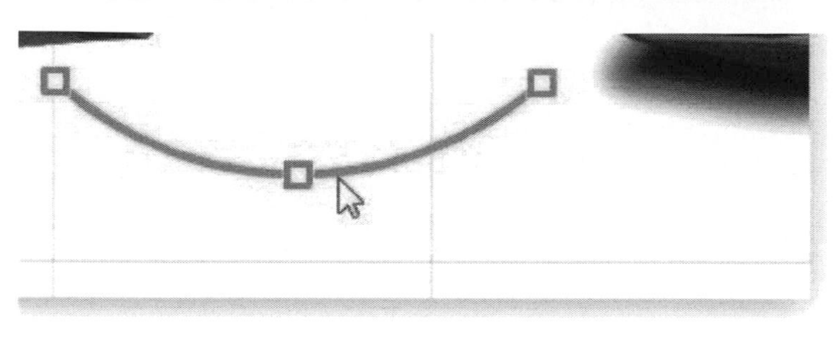

Oddly, selecting an arrow or a line doesn't produce the Transformation Tool. Instead, you get some handles. The handles at either end of a line or arrow allow you to position the start and end point; and the handle in the middle lets you bend it. Click and drag the handles as required. To *move* a line or arrow without otherwise affecting it, click anywhere apart from these handles and drag it on the canvas.

STEP 11

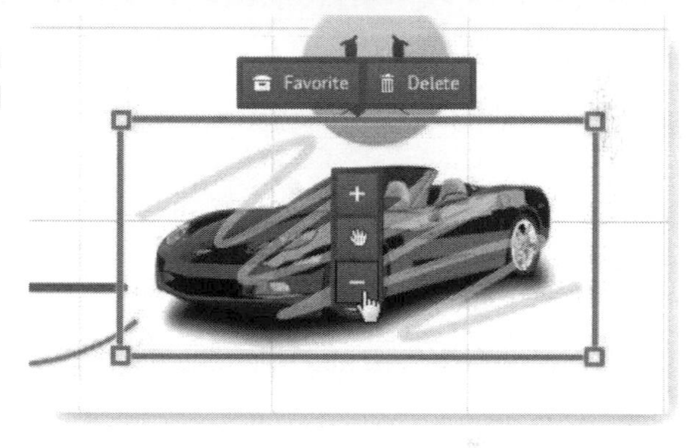

The highlighter *does* have a Transformation Tool so you can make your squiggles and scribbles bigger or smaller.

6 CUSTOMISING THEMES

Effective design requires planning and imagination. However, Prezi makes it possible to hit the ground running with a good-looking presentation. The theme governs the overall colour scheme and look of each prezi, and can be customised extensively. Getting a theme right is an excellent starting point so let's do that now.

STEP 1

Start a new blank prezi and immediately click the **Customize** button. In the sidebar on the right, you'll see theme thumbnails. Click a few of these to see the effect on the canvas and settle on something that's not a million miles from what you have in mind. Then look for the **Advanced** button at the foot of the sidebar and click this to fire up the Theme Wizard

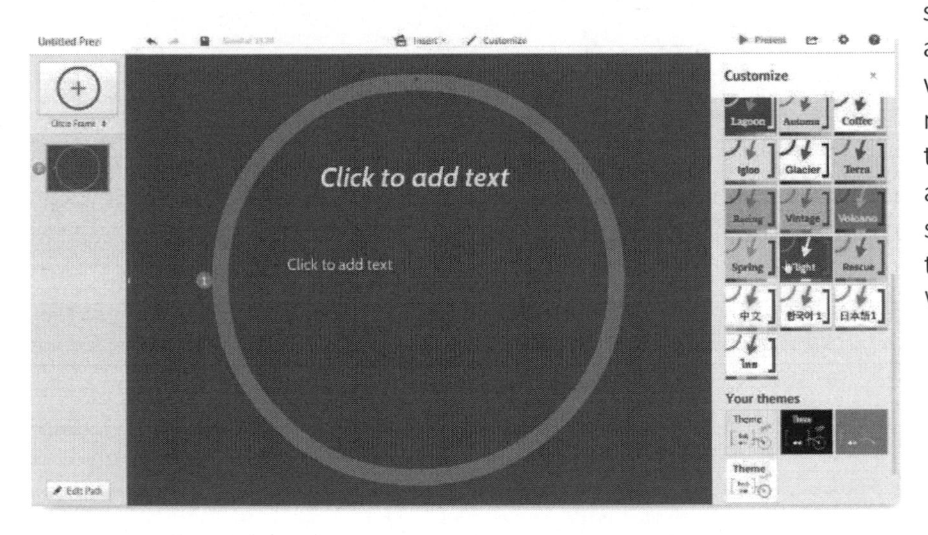

STEP 2

In **Wizard** mode, use the **Back** / **Next** buttons to explore the options. These include selecting a background colour for the canvas and different colours for lines, arrows, frames and the marker (or highlighter). As you make choices, the preview pane at the top shows the effect of your changes.

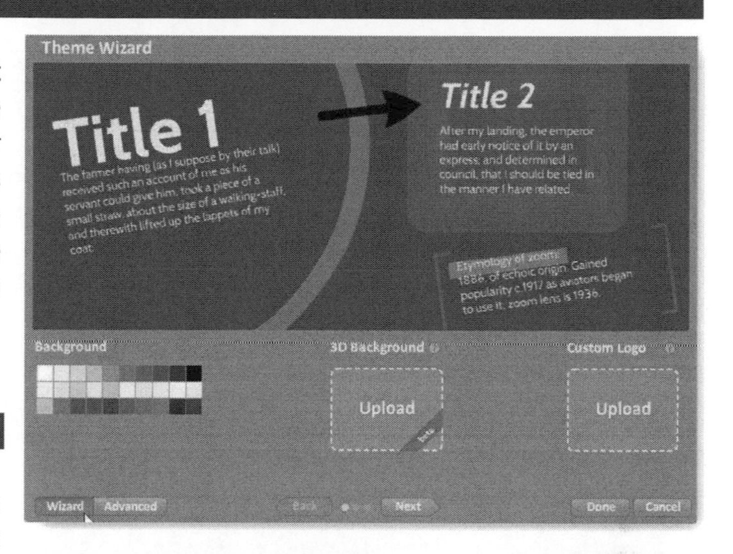

STEP 3

On the second page, you can select font styles for each of your text options: **Title**, **Subtitle** (called **Title 2** in the Theme Wizard) and **Body**. What you *can't* do is specify a font that's not included here. There are good technical reasons for this but it's a frustrating limitation. If you have brand guidelines, as any large company will, you'll want to use your corporate fonts in your prezis. But you can't. All you can do is choose something reasonably close.

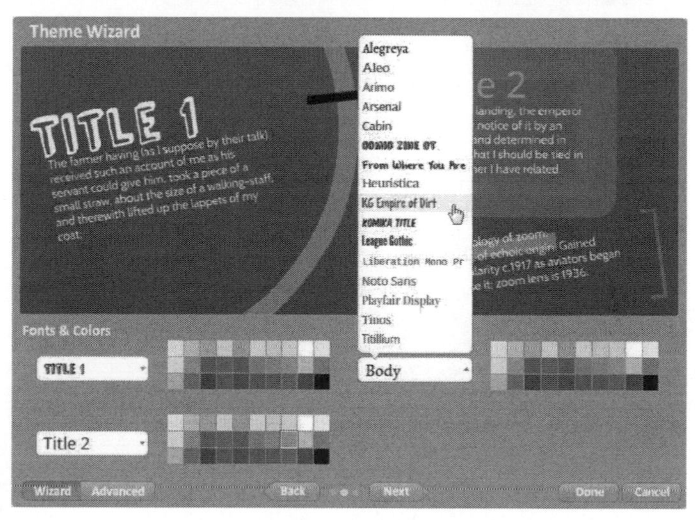

STEP 4

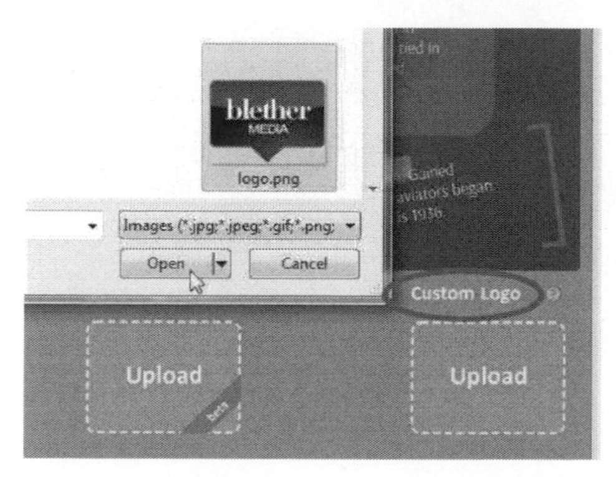

You can, however, upload your company logo. If you do so, you won't see it on the canvas until you present, at which point it will float above all other content in the bottom-left corner of the screen. This is another time when it can be useful to have a graphical logo saved as a transparent PNG file format. My logo, shown here, has a transparent background. You'll see it in Chapter 9.

STEP 5

The **Advanced** button in Theme Wizard allows you to set precise colours for all the key Prezi elements. Just plug in RGB value and away you go. If you don't know how to find RGB values, here's a great, free little tool:

www.nattyware.com/pixie.php

Open your website and use Pixie to point at any colour you want to identify. Make a note of the RGB values and plug them into the Theme Wizard.

STEP 6

When you've set up a theme that you think will work for you, exit the Theme Wizard. You can at this point save it in the **Your Themes** section of the **Customize** sidebar. You can save up to five themes here for reuse later.

A couple of comments at this juncture:

- You can edit your theme at any point when you're working on a prezi. That said, the text styles (or fonts) are all different sizes so switching a style halfway through will affect text positioning on the canvas. It's better to get your template right as soon as possible.
- Use **Title**, **Subtitle** and **Body** texts consistently in a prezi. It helps your audience understand the journey if, for example, section headings are all the same style and size and image captions are consistent.
- For 3D backgrounds, see p70-72.

7 WORKING WITH FRAMES

Frames are another key feature in Prezi. We saw a circle frame back in Step 3 on p12 and we've looked at how to choose frame colours in the Theme Wizard. But what exactly *are* frames? In fact, they have three functions:

1. **Design Elements** – Frames can be used to give visual structure to content. We'll see this on p36-37 when we look at layouts.
2. **Group content** – When objects are positioned within a frame, those objects are grouped by the frame. Resize or rotate the frame and everything inside it gets resized or rotated too.
3. **'Slides'** – Yep, you read that right. Think of frames as roughly equivalent to slides in a PowerPoint deck. This will make sense shortly when we look at the Prezi path.

Understanding how to work with frames is crucial in Prezi, because frames – together with the path – control how content is displayed during a presentation. But first a word about aspect ratio. All newish displays have a 'widescreen' aspect ratio of 16:9. If you'll be presenting on a 16:9 screen, it makes good sense to optimise your prezi to fit that screen perfectly. If, however, you might be using an older projector, chances are it will output the squarer 4:3 aspect ratio.

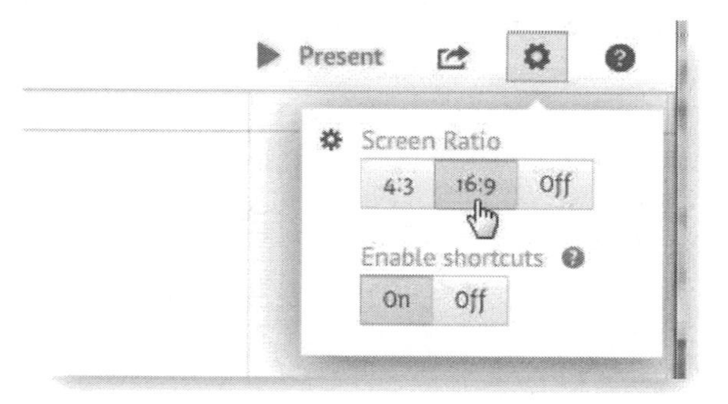

In prezi, you can set the aspect ratio for each prezi from the settings menu in the toolbar. Click the cog icon and select 4:3 or 16:9 depending on the type you screen you'll be using. If you don't know for sure, opt for 4:3. If you end up using a 16:9 screen, your prezi will

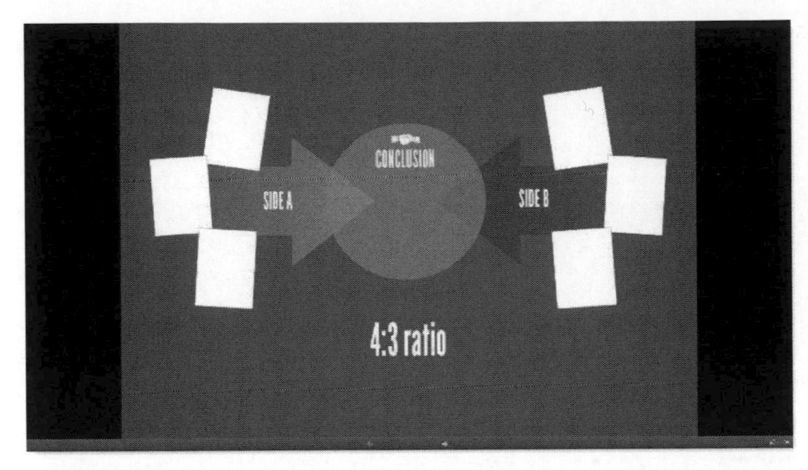

have black bands either side, as shown here. This is actually preferable to presenting a 16:9 prezi on a 4:3 screen, because then you get black bands top and bottom and the whole thing looks rather squished (just as widescreen movies looked on your old TV before you got a 16:9 flatscreen).

STEP 1

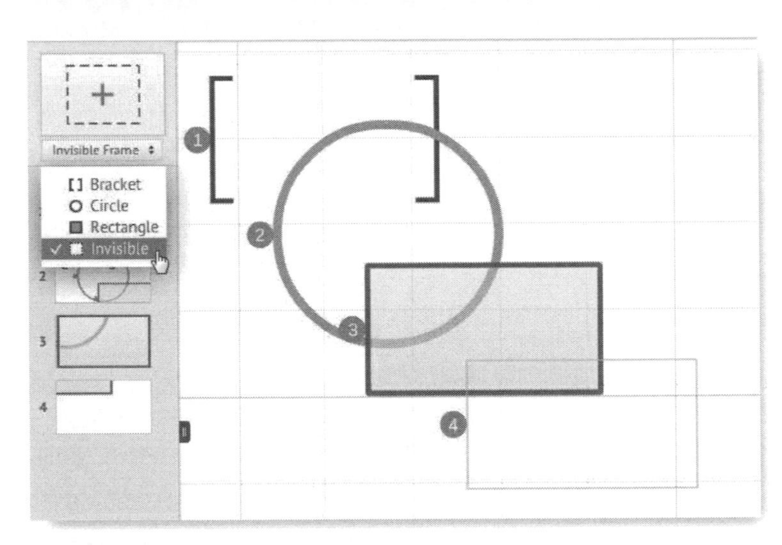

Having selected an aspect ratio, start a new, blank prezi. In the sidebar on the left, you'll find a dropdown menu with four frame styles. Select one and your choice will be shown in the preview window above the menu. Click the plus sign to add that style of frame to the canvas. Repeat for the other frame types until you have all four.

STEP 2

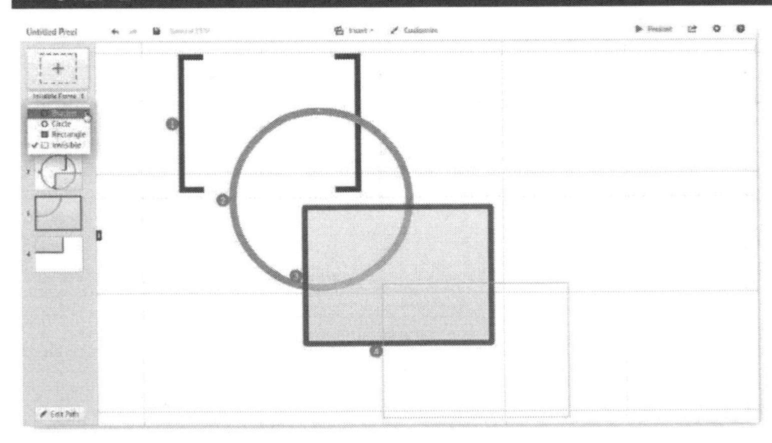

In the previous screenshot, the aspect ratio was 16:9. Here's what frames look like when the aspect ratio is 4:3. When you use a frame as a 'slide in a prezi, it will be displayed full screen. These frames would fit a 4:3 screen perfectly while those in the previous step would fit a 16:9 screen.

The first frame style, bracket, is the archetypal Prezi frame. If you've seen a dozen prezis, you've seen a hundred bracket frames. The circle frame is just a circle, and the rectangle is the same shape and aspect ratio as a bracket but has a solid border and is lightly shaded. All three of these frames are visible when used on the canvas and should be treated as elements of your design.

The last frame type is different. You use invisible frames to control and organise content just like the other frames, but the audience can't see them. If you prefer a 'clean' approach and don't want your presentations to look like everyone else's, you'll use invisible frames frequently.

STEP 3

Put a couple of symbols or shapes inside a frame. Now click carefully on the edge of the frame to select it, and note the selection box, the Transformation Tool and the menu. If you move, resize or rotate the frame, everything inside it goes along for the ride. That's because the frame has automatically grouped its contents. You can use the corner handles to scale or rotate the frame just as you can with any selected content.

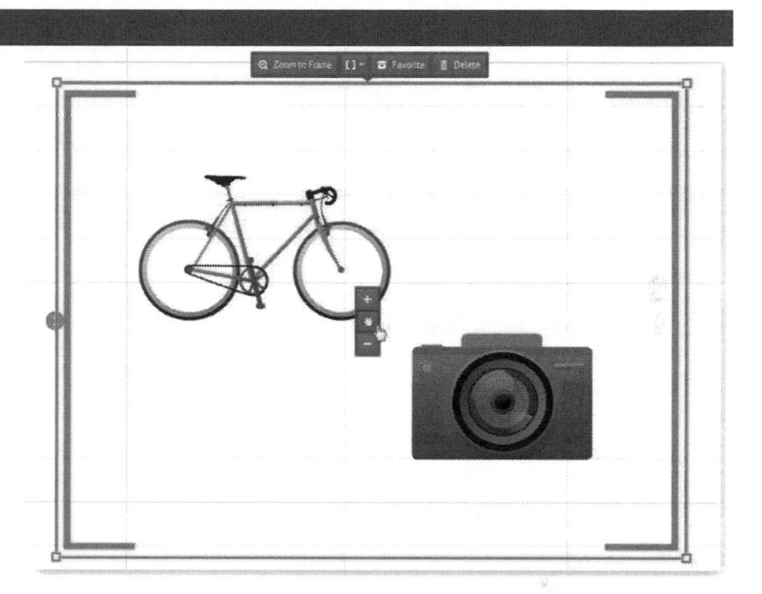

STEP 4

To remover a frame, *don't* click the **Delete** button in the toolbar! That deletes the frame *and* the grouped contents. Instead, use the frame button in the menu to either replace the current frame with a different type or to delete it from the canvas *without* deleting the objects within it.

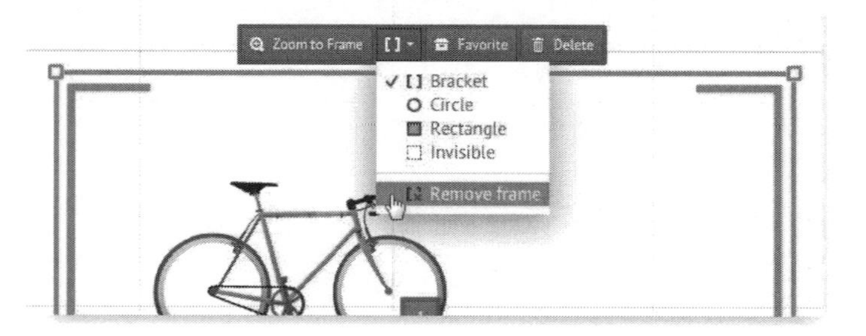

STEP 5

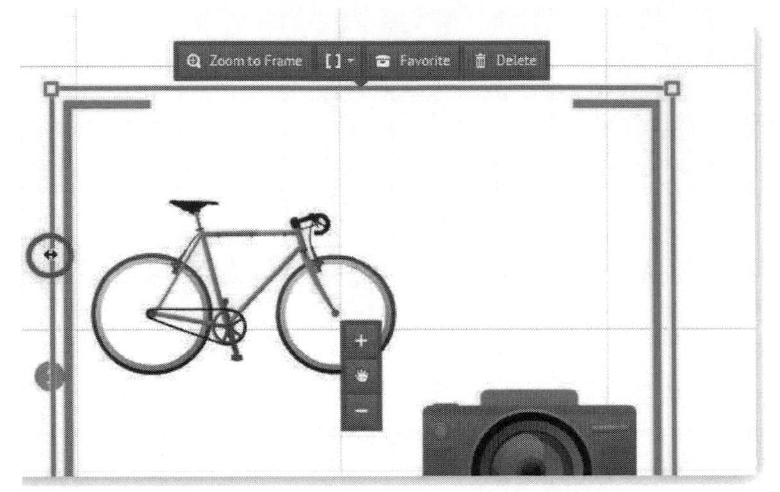

With the exception of circle frames, which are always circles, you can change the shape of a frame by selecting it and dragging the edges of the selection box. If you want a squarer frame, drag the left and right borders inwards. If you want an elongated rectangle, drag the borders outwards.

STEP 6

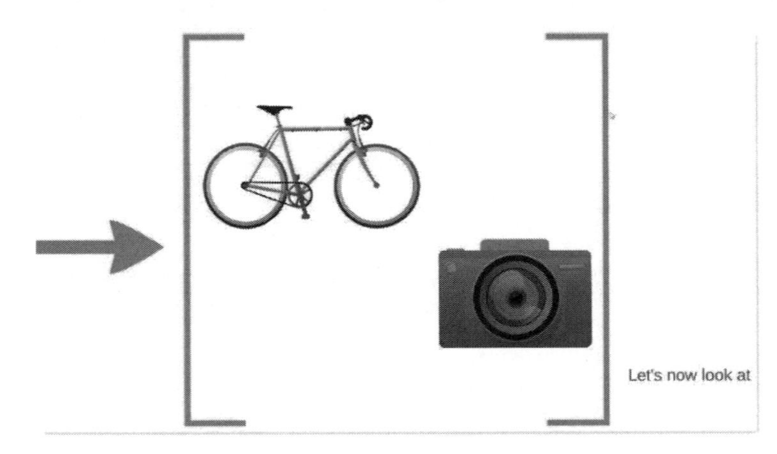

Bear in mind that changing a frame's shape will have an effect on how content is displayed. If you squeeze a 16:9 frame into a square, during presentation that frame will fit the screen top to bottom but some of the prezi canvas on either side will also be visible. If there's other content nearby, it may bleed into the display, as in this example.

STEP 7

You can either put frames on the canvas first and then add content, which is the easy way to do things, or you can put a frame around content that's already on the canvas. Practise the latter for a moment. Insert a few objects on an otherwise blank canvas, then select a frame type and add it to the canvas.

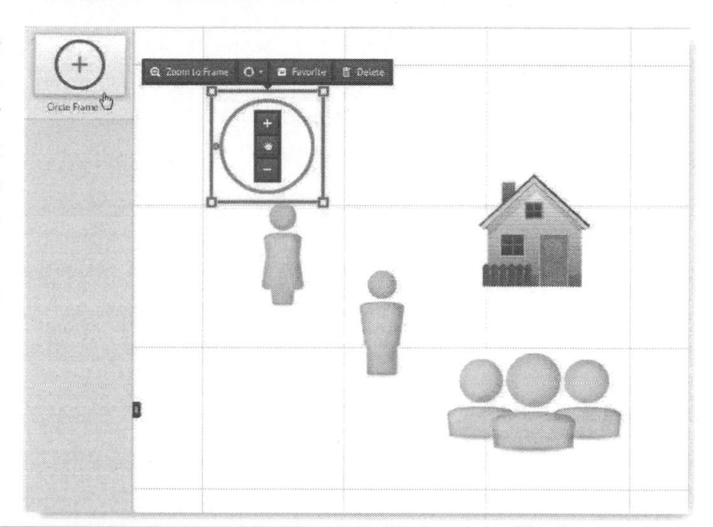

STEP 8

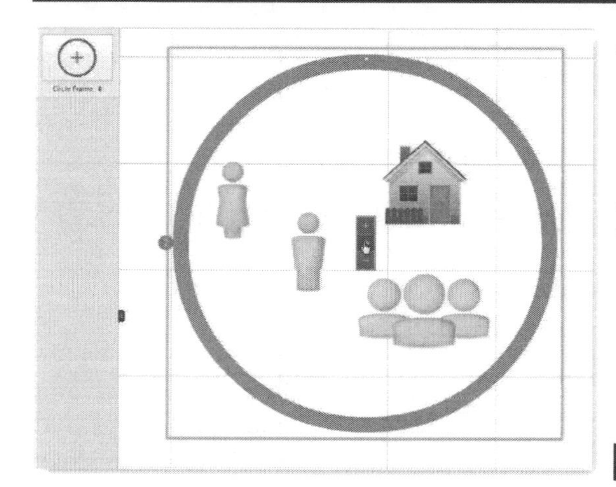

While the frame remains selected – as indicated by the selection box around it – use the plus button on the Transformation Tool or the corner handles to make the frame big enough to comfortably encompass all the other objects. Then drag it into place around them.

STEP 9

The objects will now be grouped with the frame, so if you move or otherwise change the frame, everything inside it is affected. However, you can still edit objects individually. Here, I'm making one of the figures larger without affecting the other objects. This is a key difference between grouping content with frames and grouping content manually (see p21). When content is grouped manually, you can't edit individual objects without first ungrouping the group.

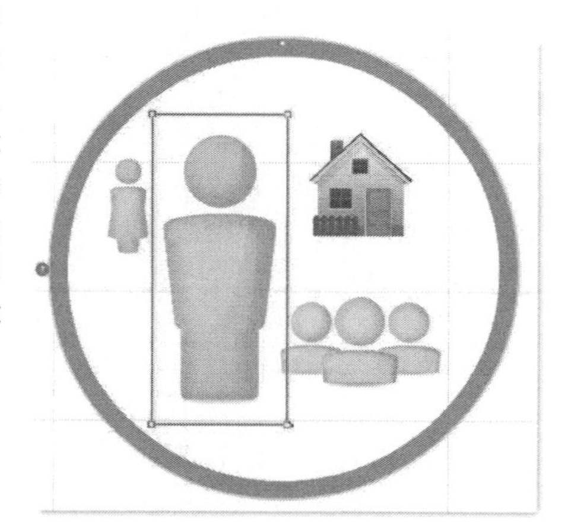

STEP 10

Remember what I said about duplicating content? You can duplicate frames *with* their contents. Select a frame and use the **Ctrl + D** keystroke combination. A duplicate will appear alongside the original, positioned on the same horizontal plane. The new frame will also be pre-selected so it's easy to move, scale or duplicate again. The objects within each frame can be individually edited.

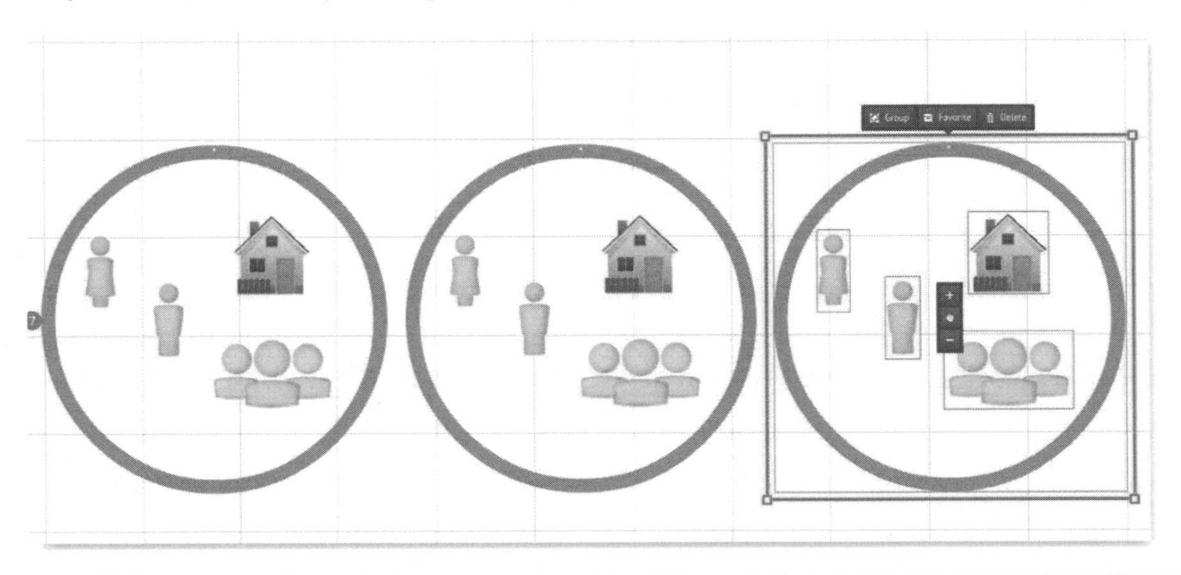

STEP 11

Because frames are so important, Prezi comes with a healthy collection of pre-configured frame layouts. You'll find these via the **Insert** menu. Here, for instance, is a single frame designed to display a couple of images and a caption. Select an image and use the **Replace** button to swap it for something of your own.

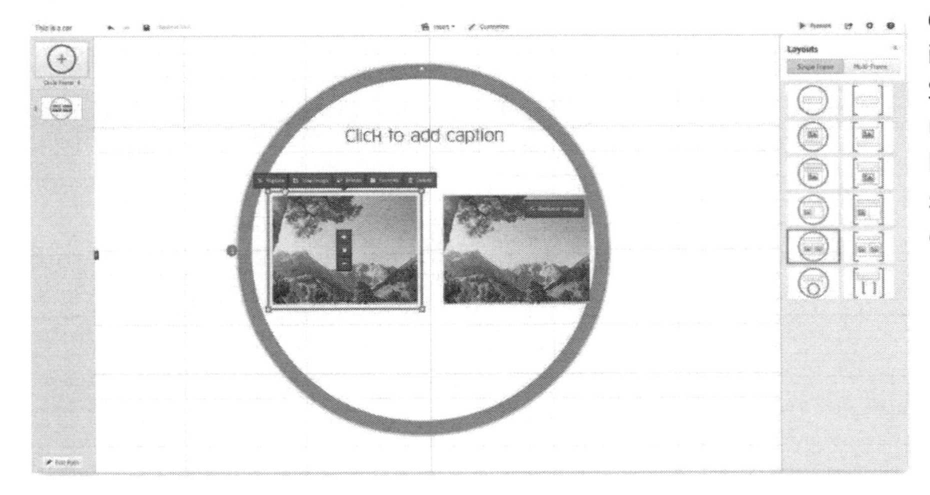

STEP 12

Here's a layout that has multiple frames and could, in fact, form the basis of an entire prezi. All you have to do is add your own content within the frames. Equally, this layout could be dropped into a larger prezi and used to illustrate, say, a company's organizational structure or product range as part of a wider story.

Layouts are great time-savers. That's why everyone uses them – and that's why a lot of the prezis you see are very similar. Death by Prezi? It's a grim thought so don't rely upon layouts at the expense of imagination.

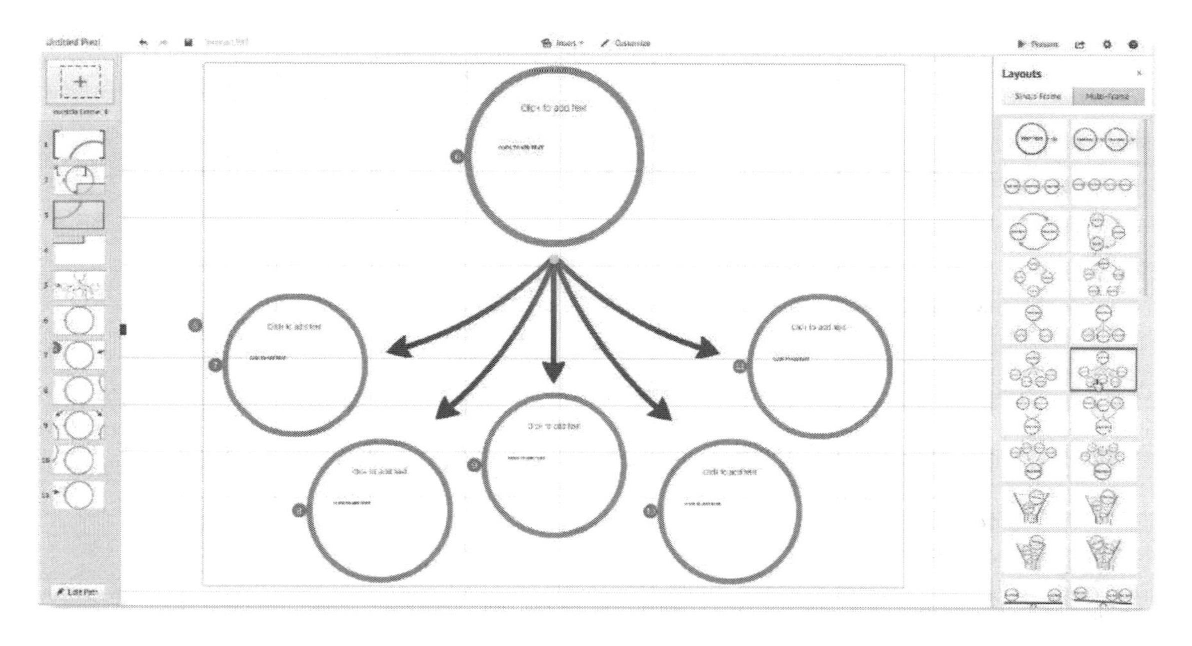

8 THE PREZI PATH

Hey, things are getting exciting! It's time to switch from editing to presenting. To do this, we need to get to grips with the path.

In PowerPoint, you have slides; in Prezi, you have path points. They're not so very different. A click on the presenter's clicker moves a presentation forward. If a PowerPoint has 16 slides, that's 16 clicks from start to finish. If a Prezi path has 16 points, ditto. (In both cases, that's excluding click-activated content *within* a slide or path point.) A slide fills the display screen. So does a path point. Both are linear journeys from beginning to end.

Of course, there are huge differences between PowerPoint and Prezi, not least that PowerPoint is entirely slide-based whereas Prezi has an expansive blank canvas to play with. But at the point of getting something on screen for your audience, and then clicking through to something else, slides and path points serve the same purpose.

Let's create a path for some random content, see it in action, and then consider how frames fit in with the path.

STEP 1

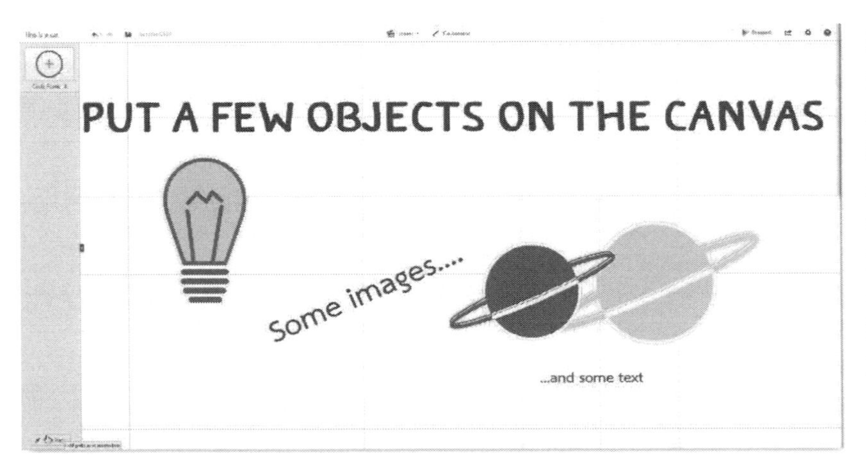

Start a new blank prezi and add a couple of lines of text and a few shapes and symbols. Overlap a couple of objects as I've done here with the two planets, or just put objects close together. Don't include any frames for now.

STEP 2

Now click the **Present** button in the toolbar. Prezi for Windows switches from Edit mode, which is where we've been all this time, to Present mode. Gone are the editing tools. What you see now is what your audience will see. If you uploaded a logo (Step 4 on p29), you'll see it here, too.

Thing is, you can't do very much with a prezi like this. You can move the canvas around with your mouse and you can click on any object to zoom in on it, but this isn't exactly a presenter-friendly experience. You'll want to be able to click your way through the canvas from one point to the next. Hit **Escape** to return to Edit mode.

STEP 3

At the foot of the left-hand sidebar, you'll find a button called **Edit Path**. Click this. Now work your way around the canvas clicking on each object in turn. Go in any order you like. Each time you click, you'll see a number appear next to the object. This is a path point

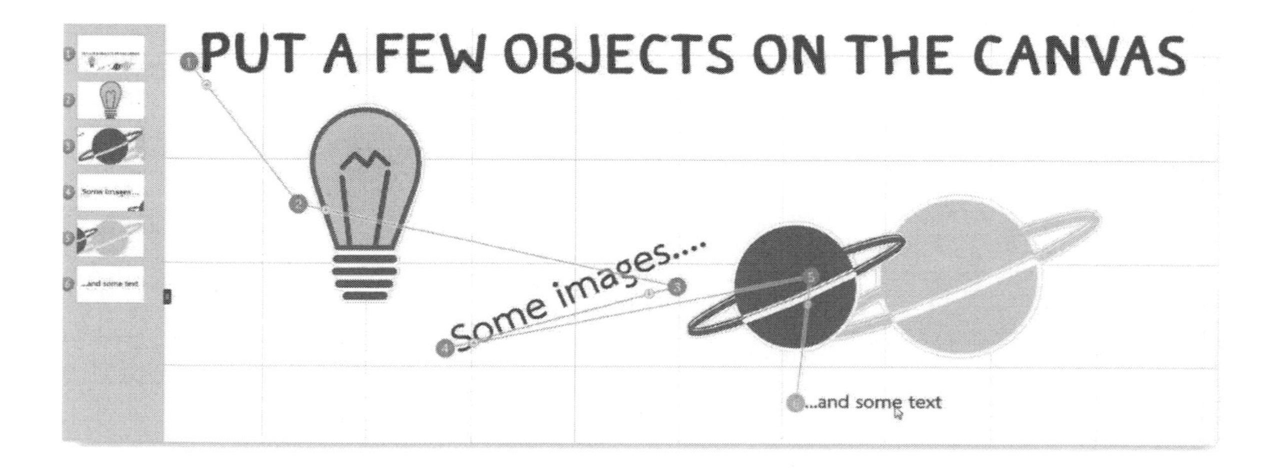

STEP 4

The numbers on the canvas – the path points – are connected by a line. This is the path. In the sidebar, each path point is represented by a thumbnail. You can drag these path points into a new order in the sidebar, and the path on the canvas will update dynamically.

What you've just done, essentially, is make some slides. Now click **Present** again and use your keyboard arrows to play your presentation. Remember, this is exactly how it will look to your audience. Here's what my path looks like when presented.

Note how the lightbulb is displayed by itself, full-screen. Note how each of the two planets are centred in their respective path points, but because they overlap on the canvas they overlap during presentation. Note how the text is displayed full-screen, which loses the difference in scale on the canvas. And you can see one of the planets encroaching on the **Some images** path point...

It's all a bit of a mess, quite frankly, with the presentation jumping from one full-screen object to another! The trouble is that Prezi *always* displays path points full-screen, and each of my path points is a single object. We need more control. We need frames.

STEP 5

Let's cheat for a moment. Open a new prezi and insert one of the complex layouts we looked at earlier (Step 12 on p37). Layouts come with paths built-in so you can switch to Present mode and click your way through a fully fledged presentation.

Here's a timeline layout with 6 path points. The first path point is a frame (an invisible one, as it happens) around the entire timeline. Path point #2 is a bracket frame connected to year 2001, path point #3 is an identical frame for 2004, and so on. When presented, the prezi begins with an overview of the whole timeline – path point #1 – and then zooms in on the canvas to show each bracket frame full-screen in sequence. These frames are 16:9 so if you play the prezi on a 16:9 display, the frames will fill the screen perfectly.

Within each frame could be... well, anything at all. Text, images, videos, diagrams, and anything else that tells the story of that year. The point is that frames plus the path give you complete control over your presentation from start to finish.

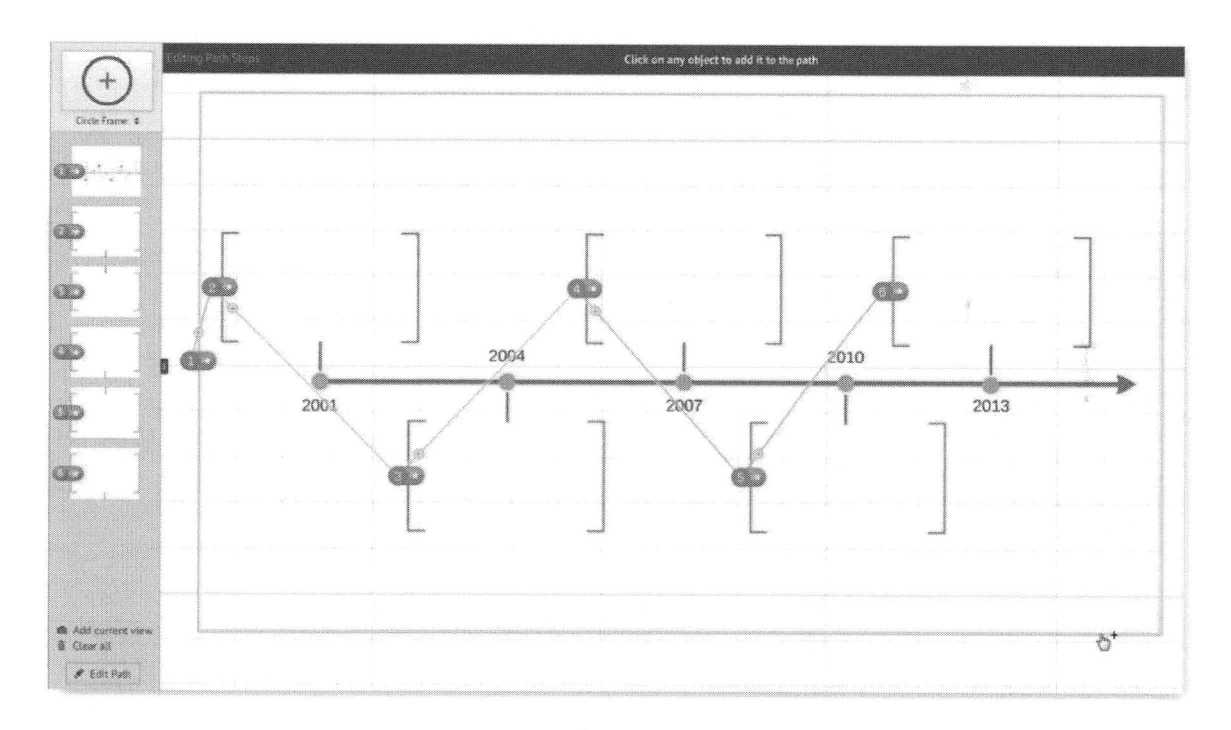

STEP 6

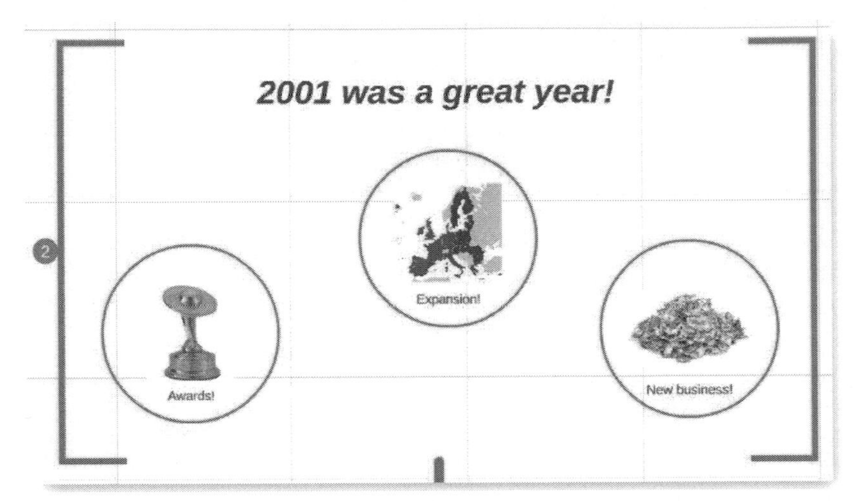

It's perfectly possible to add intermediary path points. Path point #1, for instance, might hold a lot of content that you'd want to examine sequentially.

Add some sample content and enclose it within frames. I'm using circle frames here to illustrate why they're problematic.

STEP 7

Now switch on **Edit Path** again (see Step 3 on p39) and click each of the new frames in order. Be sure to click the *frame*, not any content within it. The new frames will become path points at the end of the prezi path, so that's #7, #8 and #9 here.

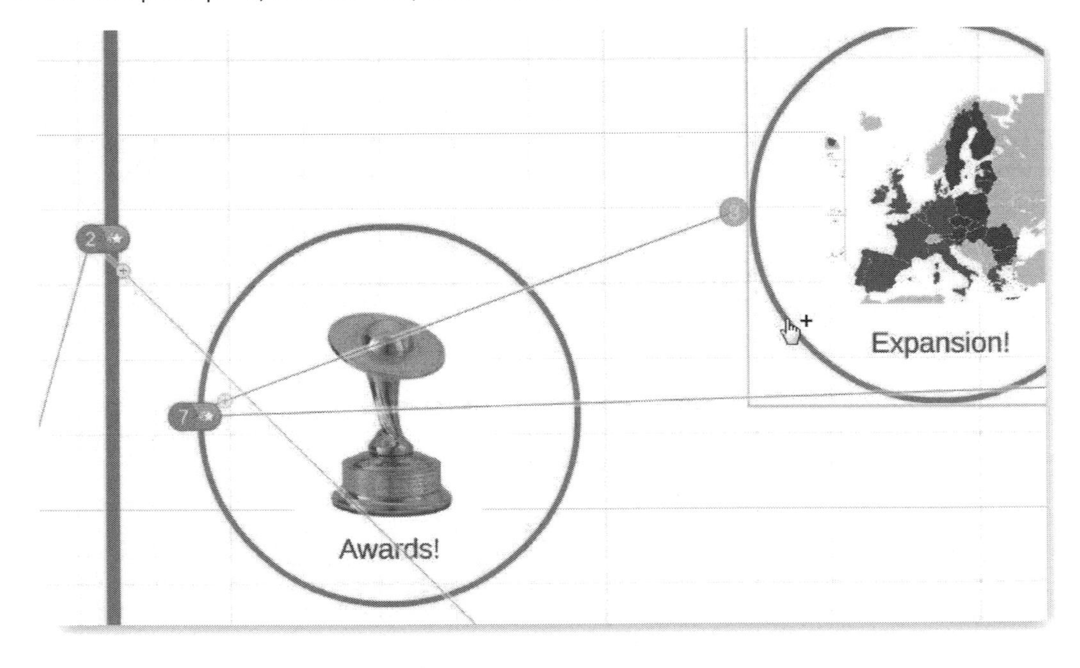

STEP 8

Back in the path sidebar, we need to figure out the correct path order. In this example, I want the prezi to run in this sequence:

Path point #1: Show the overview of the whole timeline
Path point #2: Zoom in on the bracket frame for year 2001
Path point #3: Zoom in on the circle frame for Awards!
Path point #4: Move to the next circle frame, Expansion!
Path point #5: Move to the next circle frame, New business!
Path point #6: Move to the bracket frame for year 2004... and continue from there

So I need to drag and drop the thumbnails for #7, #8 and #9, into positions #3, #4 and #5 respectively. Here's the effect of that when I switch back to Present mode and play the prezi.

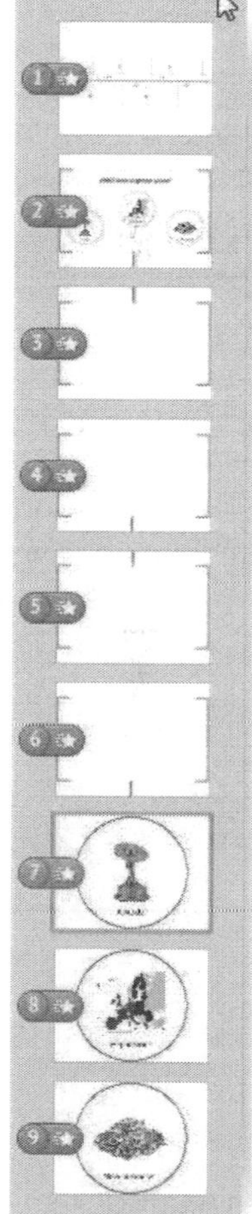

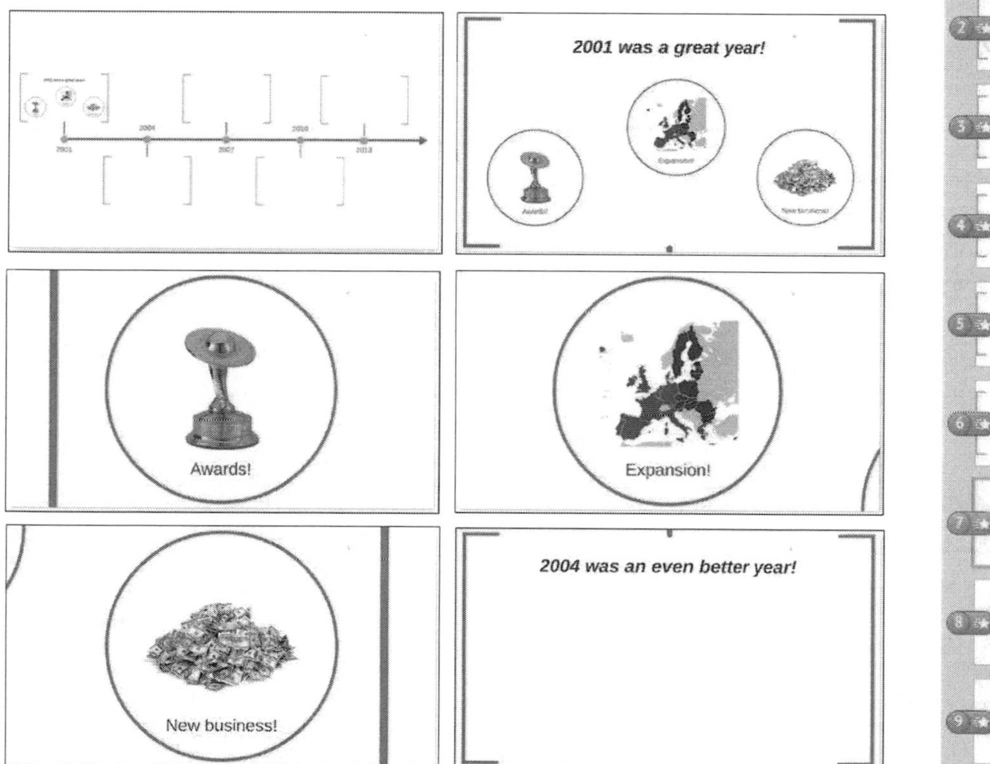

Note that there's still some irritating content overlap with the circle frames, simply because there's space either side on the 16:9 display. I could have avoided that by using bracket, rectangle or invisible frames, as these would have filled the screen completely just like path points #1, #2 and #6 above.

9 PUTTING IT ALL TOGETHER

It's time to create a prezi from scratch. What follows is a step-by-step guide to making a very simple presentation that nevertheless includes all the main ingredients you'll need to design advanced projects in Prezi.

STEP 1

You know the drill: start a new prezi with a blank canvas, select an aspect ratio (I'm going for 16:9 here) and, if you like, choose and customise a theme and upload a logo. Now put a bracket frame on the canvas and use the Transformation Tool to make it larger (or alternatively zoom in on it). Note how the new frame becomes path point #1 in the sidebar. Prezi does this automatically when you add frames.

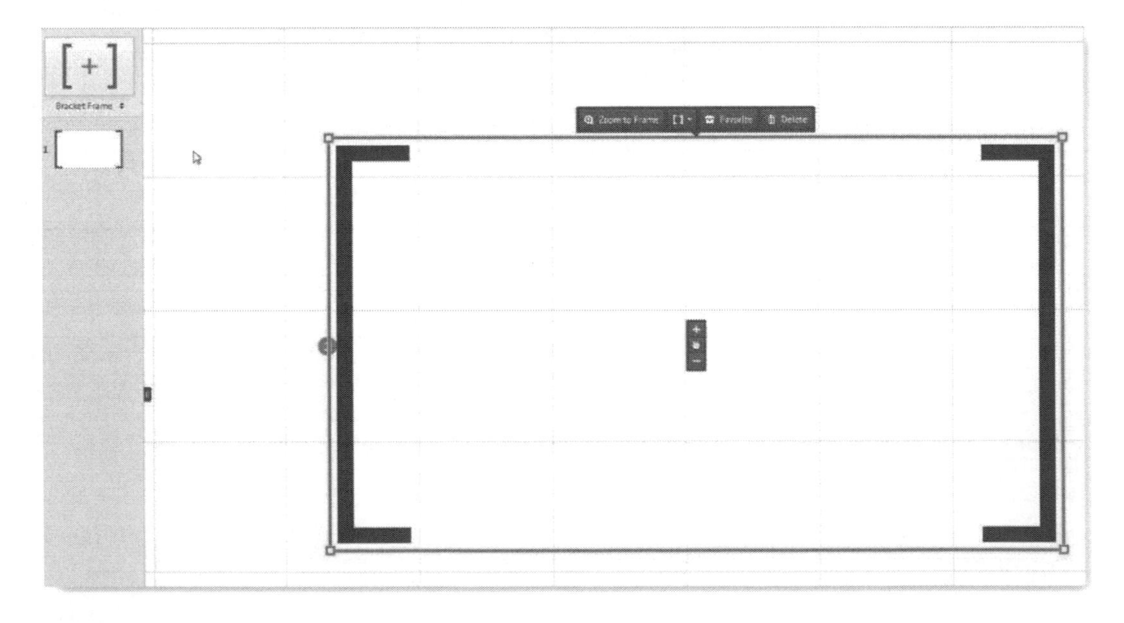

STEP 2

Click anywhere within the frame and type **Cats**. This is now a text object. Select it and use the Transformation Tool to make it bigger. Move it towards the top of the frame and aim for the middle horizontally. As you drag the object, look for a vertical dotted line. When this appears, you know that the object is centred within the frame. Leave it there.

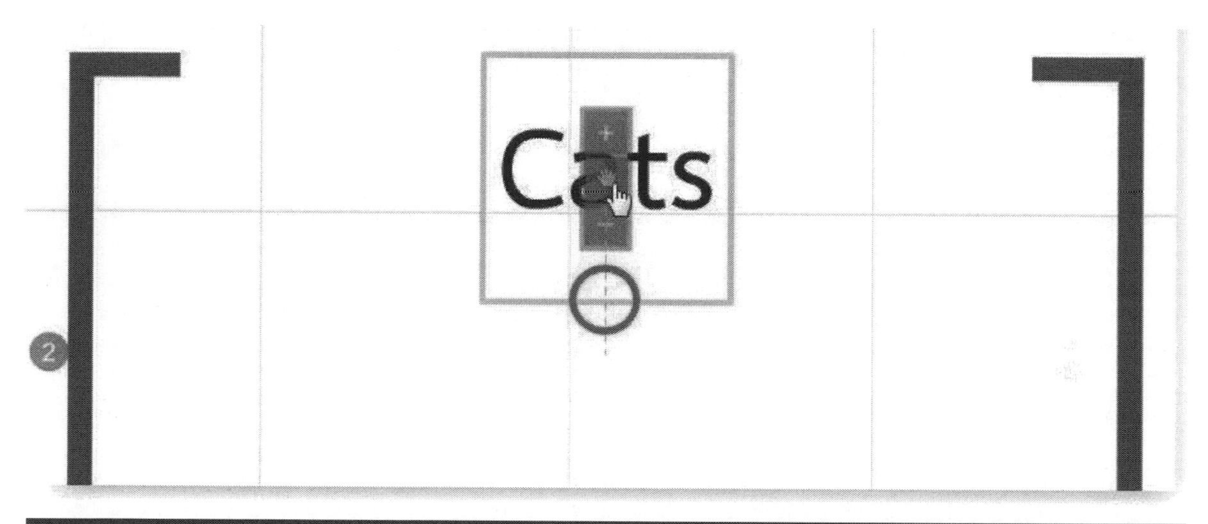

STEP 3

Now use the **Insert** menu to find a picture of a cat. Any cat will do. Position it below the title in the middle of the frame. Cute, you've made a cat slide.

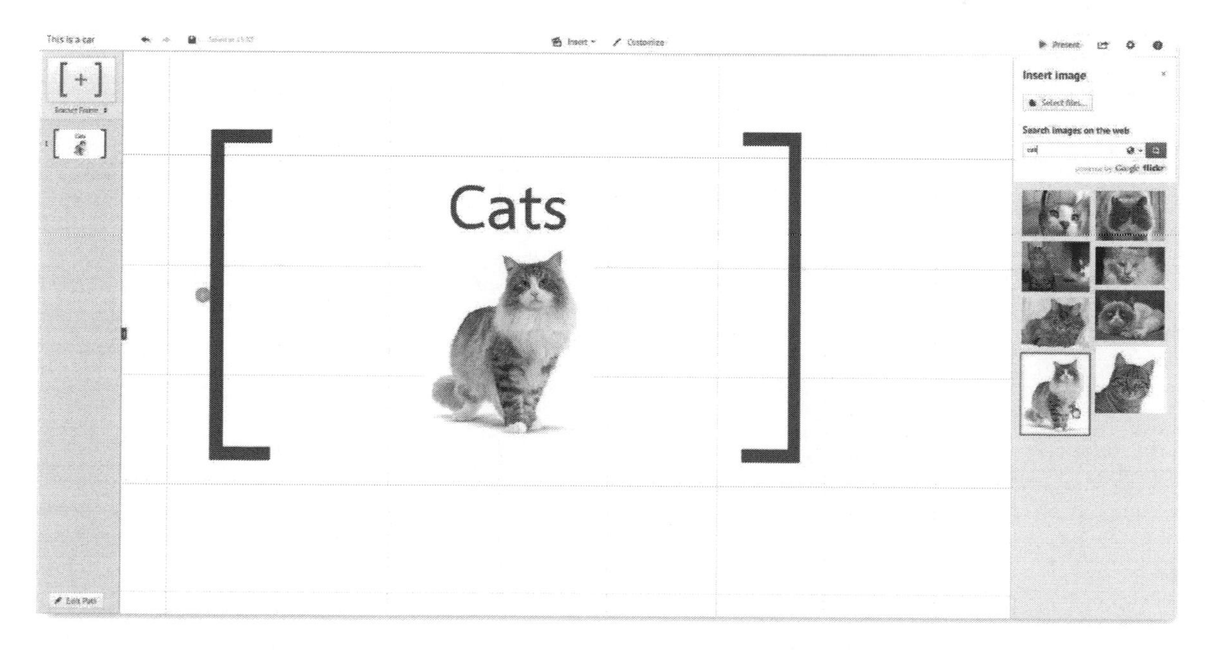

STEP 4

The next step is to make a dog slide. Start by duplicating the cat frame. Select the frame and hit **Ctrl + D**. A copy will appear alongside the original. It will already be selected and now we need to shunt it along to the right. The easiest way to do this is to use the right arrow on your keyboard while the frame remains selected. This will slide it along the canvas without moving it up or down, so your two frames remain aligned on the same horizontal plane.

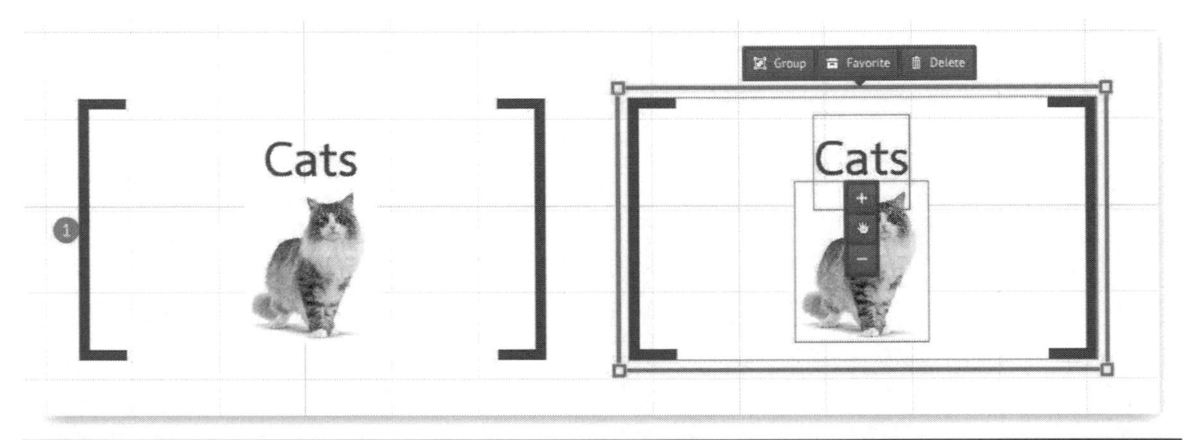

STEP 5

Now click the word **Cats** in the *new* frame, and click **Edit Text**. Change the text to, yes, **Dogs**.

STEP 6

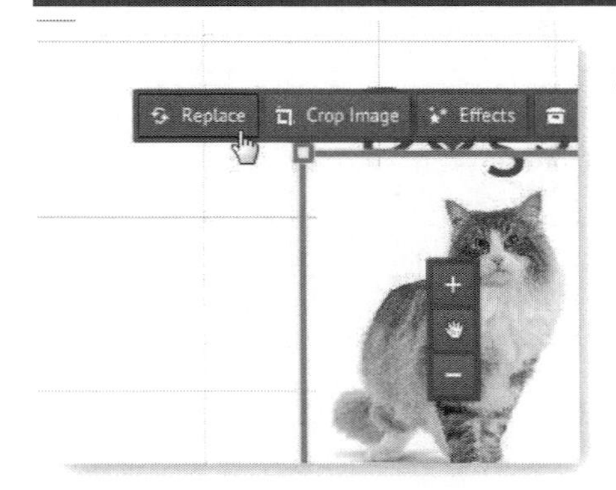

Select the cat picture and click **Replace**.

STEP 7

Search for a picture of a dog and click **Replace** in the insert image sidebar.

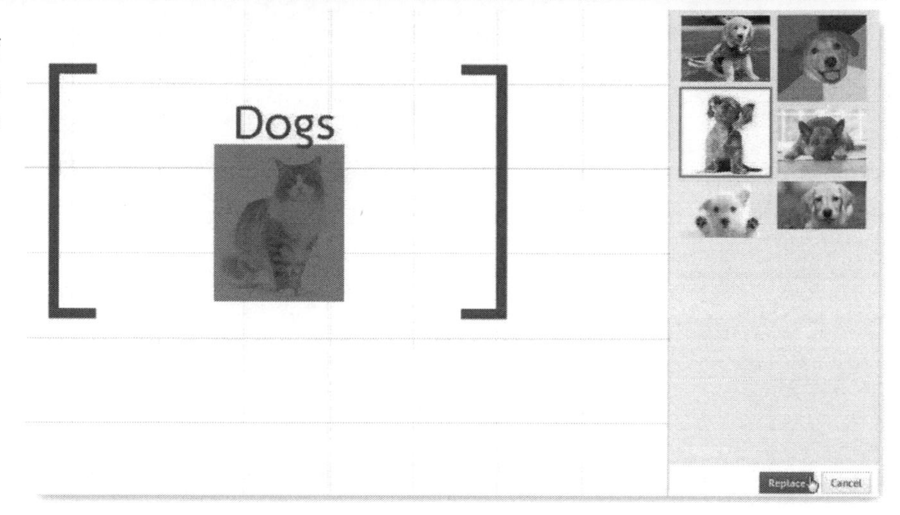

STEP 8

You should now have two frames side-by-side, one called Cats and one called Dogs, with appropriate images in each. Zoom out on the canvas (see Step 7 on p14) until you can see them both with lots of free space around them. Click on the canvas above the frames and type HOUSEHOLD PETS. Use the Transformation Tool to make this text really big, and centre it above the Cats and Dogs frames like this.

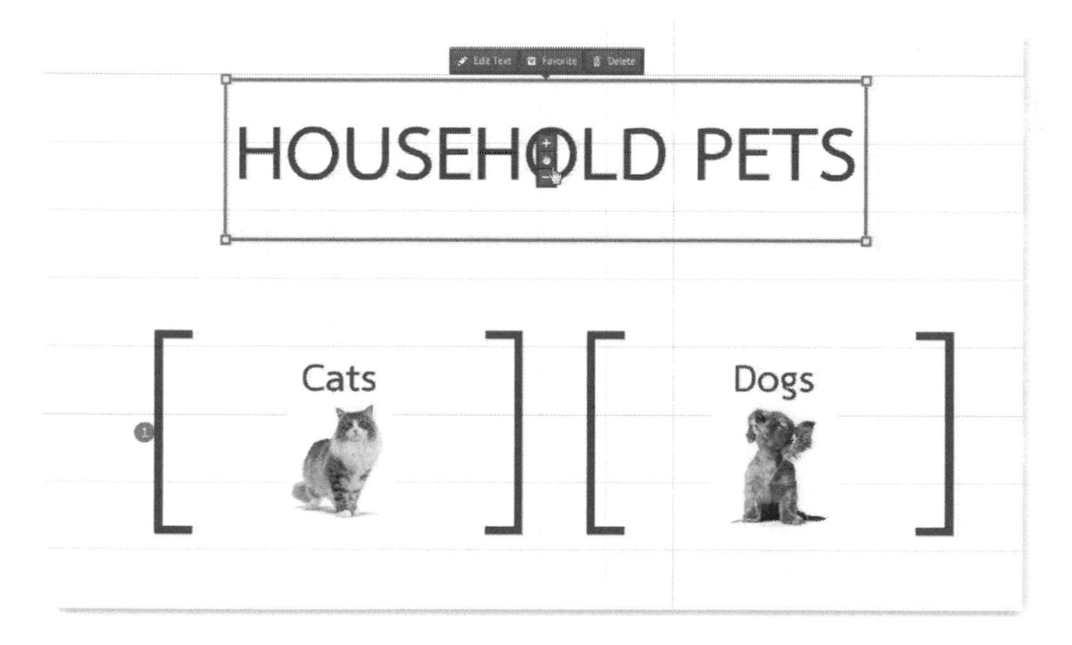

STEP 9

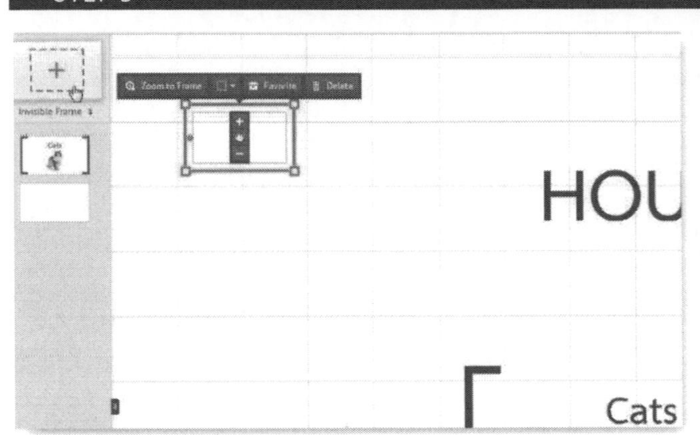

Now select the invisible frame type from the frames sidebar and add one to the canvas. Zoom right out on the canvas and scale up the invisible frame until it's big enough to fit comfortably around the other content. Use the plus/minus buttons on the Transformation Tool or the corner handles for this

STEP 10

Important! While the hidden frame is selected, you can resize it and move it around at will. But if you deselect it by clicking away, it will automatically group whatever content it happens to contain at that point, and thereafter you can't move or scale it without affecting that content. Your mission is to positon the frame around everything else like this *before* you deselect it.

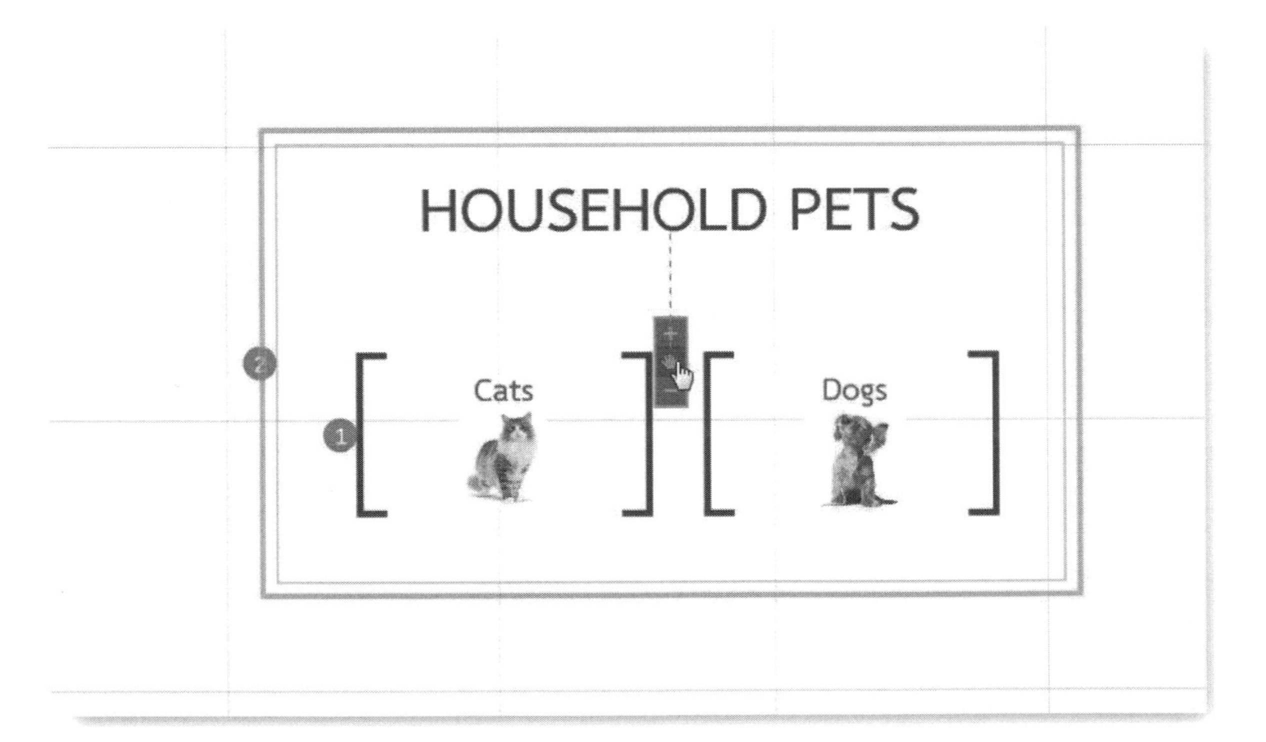

STEP 11

Right, let's turn all this effort into a presentation. At the foot of the path sidebar, click **Edit Path** followed by **Clear all**. As we just saw, Prezi automatically creates path points for new frames, but it's sometimes easier to create a path from scratch. Here's what to do:

- Click an outside edge of the hidden frame to make it path point #1
- Click an outside edge of the Cats frame to make it path point #2
- Click an outside edge of the Dogs frame to make it path point #3
- Click an outside edge of the hidden frame to make it path point #4

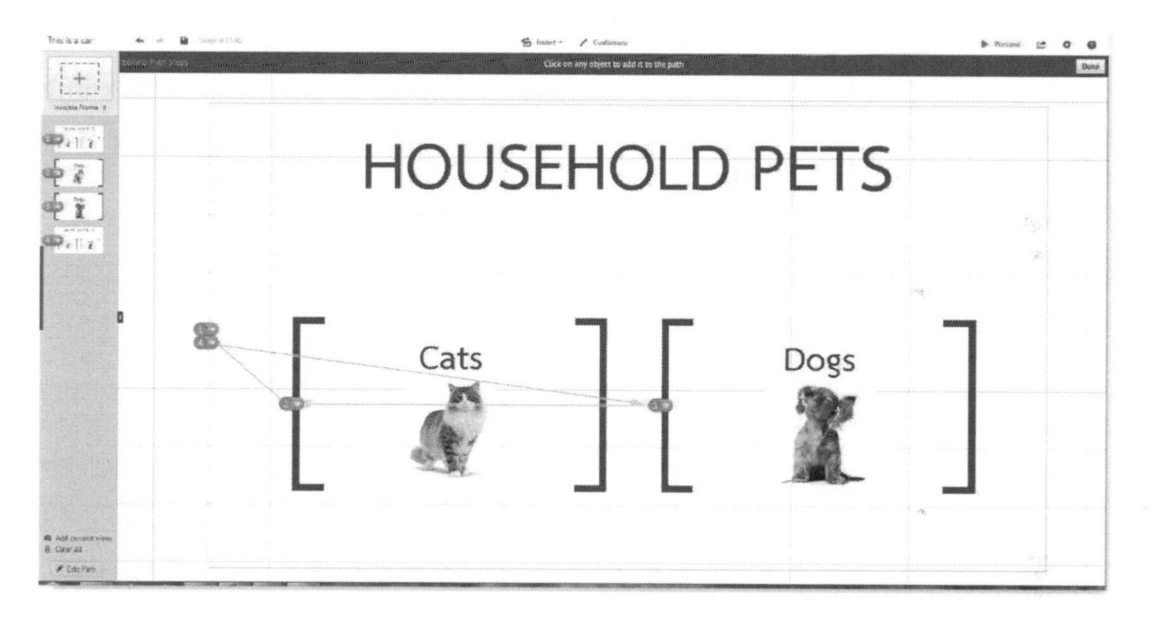

STEP 12

Now click **Present** in the toolbar and use your keyboard arrows to run through your prezi. You should have four 'slides' that look like this. Note how the bracket frames fill the screen when you present, so there's no danger of other content on the canvas overlapping.

STEP 13

The opening overview screen shows the audience what you're going to talk about (household pets), then you talk about the subject in two separate sections (cats and dogs), and then you return to the overview to remind the audience of the bigger picture. Huzzah! Have a cup of coffee. You've just created and presented a pretty reasonable prezi – which I reckon is far more than most newcomers to Prezi ever achieve.

When you're ready, let's 'Prezify' it a bit.

STEP 14

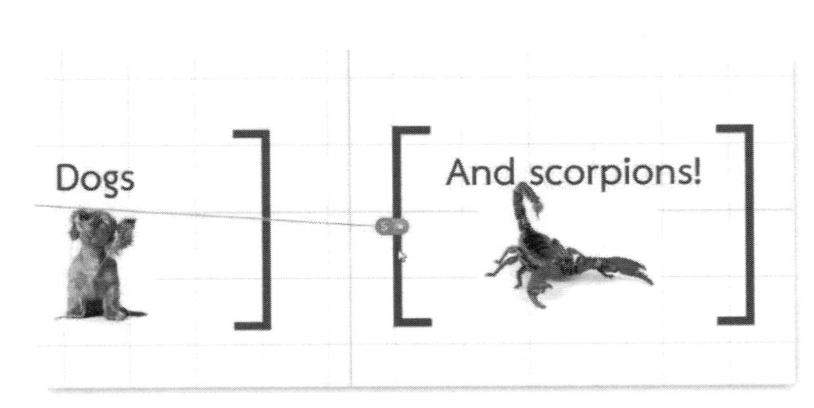

Select the Dogs frame and use **Ctrl + D** to duplicate it. Now edit the text to say **And scorpions!**. You'll need to centre this longer title in the frame. Replace the dog pic with a scorpion pic.

The new frame will automatically become path point #5, which is fine.

STEP 15

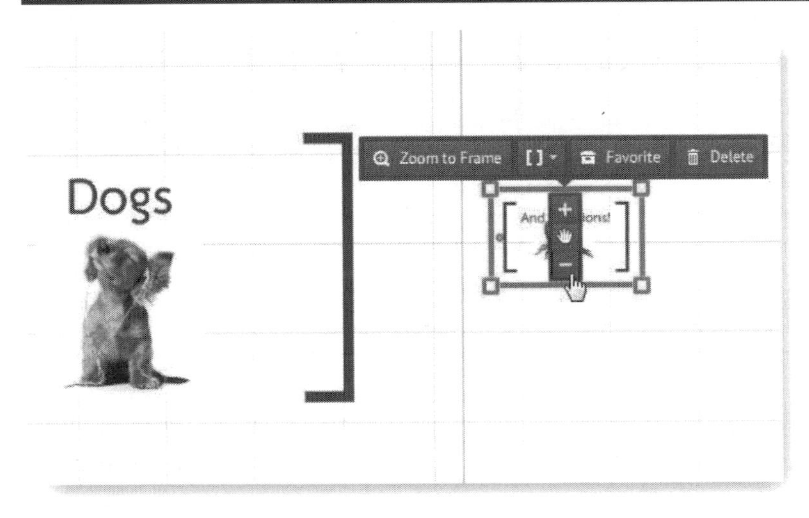

Now select the Scorpions frame and use the Transformation Tool to shrink it. When it's about significantly smaller than the Dogs frame, drag it towards the HOUSEHOLD PETS caption. Don't deselect it!

STEP 16

Once you've moved the Scorpions frame close to the title, shrink it some more. And some more. When it's tiny, drag it into the middle of the second O in the word HOUSEHOLD. You'll have to zoom in on the canvas to do this accurately. When it's in place, deselect it by clicking away, and zoom back out on the canvas.

STEP 17

Finally, return to **Edit Path** and click the overview frame to make it path point #6. The full order should then be:

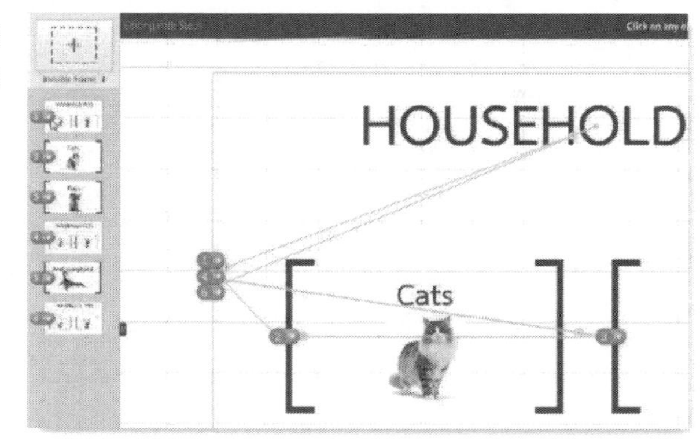

- Path point #1: Overview frame
- Path point #2: Cats frame
- Path point #3: Dogs frame
- Path point #4: Overview frame
- Path point #5: Scorpions frame
- Path point #6: Overview frame

What we've just done is hide the scorpion on the canvas. It's so small that the audience can't see it when you present. When you get to path point #4, it will seem that your story is complete. But with the very next click, the prezi will zoom right through the word HOUSEHOLD and fill the screen with the scorpion. Cue shock! Cue general hilarity! Point made, your next click takes the audience back to the overview, and your scorpion shrinks back out of sight.

This hidden reveal technique is commonly used in Prezi. In fact, it's overused. However, when the circumstances justify hiding and dramatically revealing a part of the story, it *can* be effective.

STEP 16

Here's what it should look like (although of course you can't appreciate the zoom effect when it's laid out like this). In the next chapter, we're going to continue working with this prezi, so don't delete it yet.

10 FADE-IN ANIMATION

When Prezi first launched, the only ways to introduce new content were by zooming, as we just did with the scorpion frame, or by using the path and frames to pan to a different part of the canvas. However, from the audience's perspective, a pan is seldom a smooth motion from one frame to the next, unless the frames are very close together. More usually, Prezi pulls out from the current frame, swoops across the canvas, and zooms in again. This 'bouncing camera' effect can induce a kind of sea-sickness. It's also plain tiresome.

That's why 'fade-in animation' (awkward name for a cool feature) is so welcome. Within a frame, but *only* within a frame, you can introduce new content with a click. No movement on the canvas required.

STEP 1

Start with your HOUSEHOLD PETS prezi exactly as you left it. Click **Edit Path** and note how the path points have little stars next to them in the sidebar. Each of these path points is a frame so the contents can be animated. Click the animation star on path point #1 to open that frame in the animation window.

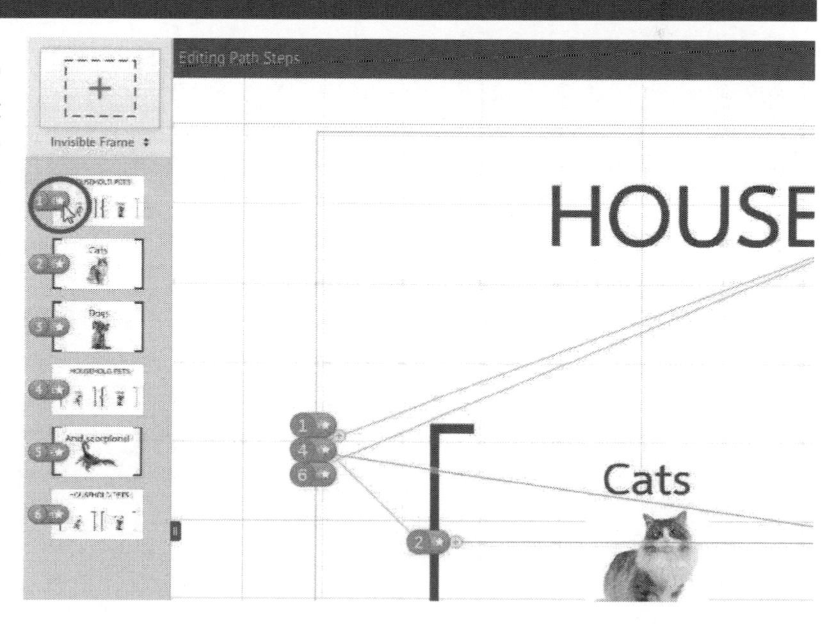

STEP 2

Very carefully, click the Cats bracket frame. You should see a green #1 appear next to the frame. Now click the Dogs frame to make it animation point #2. Click the **Play** button in the top toolbar (next to **Done**) to see the effect. What should happen is this:

- The frame is initially blank apart from the HOUSEHOLD PETS title
- The Cats frame appears
- The Dogs frame appears

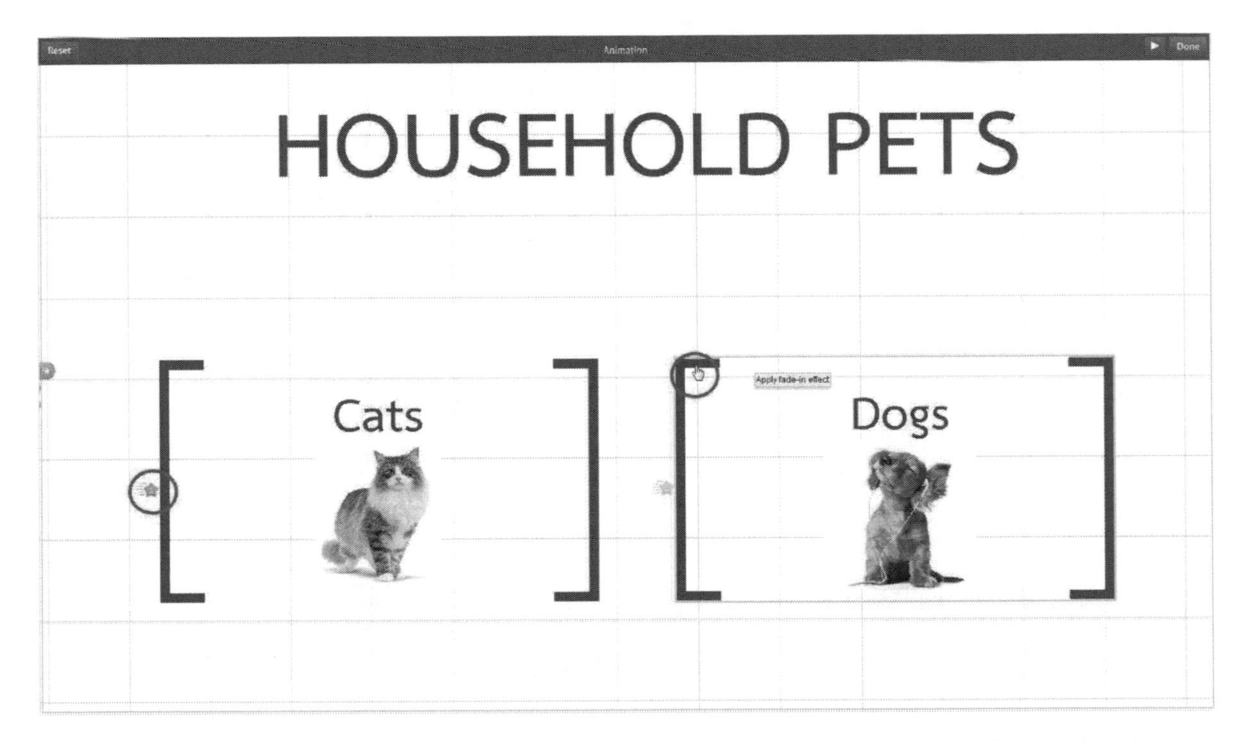

STEP 3

Click **Done** in the animation window and switch your prezi to **Present** mode. Now you should find that the opening sequence looks like this. It takes one click to make the Cats frame appear, and another to make Dogs appear. Note that you haven't created any new path points: this is simply fade-in animation applied *within* the first path point.

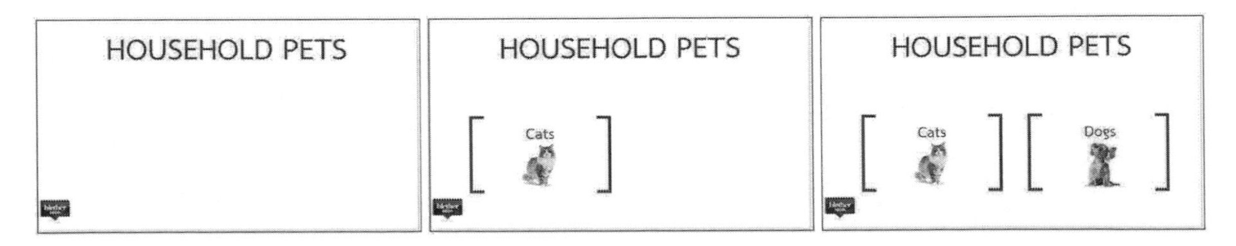

STEP 4

In the above example, you can imagine the speaker's narrative.

HOUSEHOLD PETS is on screen

So today we're going to talk about household pets. Specifically...

Click – the Cats frame appears

cats, and also...

Click – the Dogs frame appears

dogs.

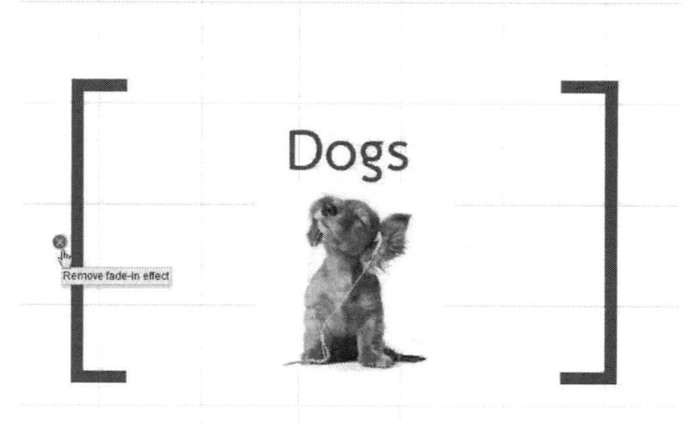

The next click takes the prezi to path point #2, the Cats frame. The speaker's up and running.

But what if you wanted to do something different and talk about cats in detail before even *mentioning* dogs? Here's how to do that.

Click **Edit Path** in the sidebar and click the animation star on path point #1 (just as in Step 1 above). Now remove the animation for the Dogs frame by hovering over the green #2 and clicking the red cross. Leave the Cats frame animated

STEP 5

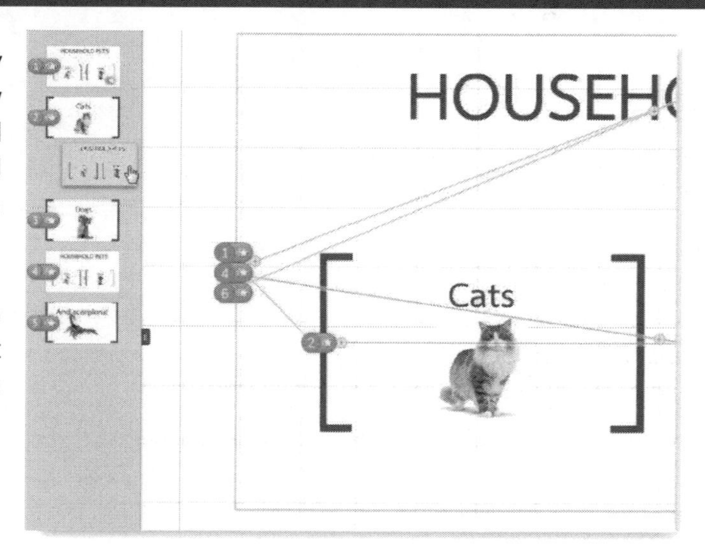

Now, in the path sidebar, carefully drag path point #6 – the overview frame at the end of the prezi – and drop it between the Cats frame and the Dogs frame. It will become path point #3.

This done, click the overview frame on the canvas. This will make it path point #7 right at the end, replacing path point #6 that you moved.

STEP 6

Your path should now be:

- Path point #1: Overview frame (with fade in animation for the Cats frame)
- Path point #2: Cats frame
- Path point #3: Overview frame
- Path point #4: Dogs frame
- Path point #5: Overview frame
- Path point #6: Scorpion frame
- Path point #7: Overview frame

All you have to do now is animate the Dogs frame in path point #3. Click the animation star next to path point #3 and click the Dogs frame.

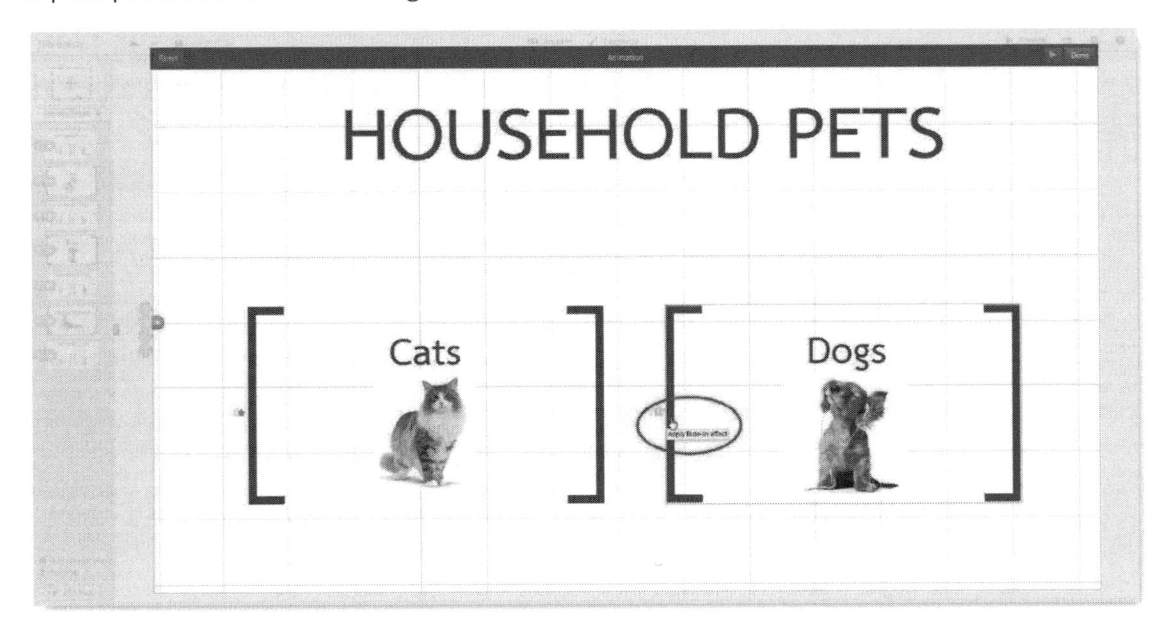

Flip your prezi into **Present** mode and confirm that your *click* sequence is as follows:

- Opens with the HOUSEHOLD PETS title and nothing else - path point #1
- Click #1: Cats frame fades in - still path point #1
- Click #2: Zoom to Cats frame - path point #2
- Click #3: Zoom back out to overview frame - path point #3
- Click #4: Dogs frame fades in - still path point #3
- Click #5: Zoom to Dogs frame - path point #4
- Click #6: Zoom back out to Overview frame - path point #5
- Click #7: Zoom in on Scorpions frame - path point #6
- Click #8: Zoom back out to Overview frame - path point #7

STEP 7

Ok, now we've turned our simple pets prezi into something rather more complex. It incorporates:

- Frames
- A path
- Fade-in animation within path points
- Zoom to frames
- Zoom to a hidden reveal (the Scorpions frame)

Let's take things one stage further by adding some additional animation within the animal frames. On your canvas, zoom in on the Cats frame. Use the **Insert** > **Symbols and Shapes** menu to find a speech bubble and drag it next to the cat picture. Now click within the speech bubble and type miaow (just a suggestions). Resize the bubble and text appropriately.

STEP 8

Now you need to group the bubble and the text. As before (see Step 8 on p21), click the text to select it, then hold down the **Ctrl** key and click the bubble. Now click **Group**.

STEP 9

Once grouped, select the bubble/text grouped object and make a duplicate (**Ctrl + D**).

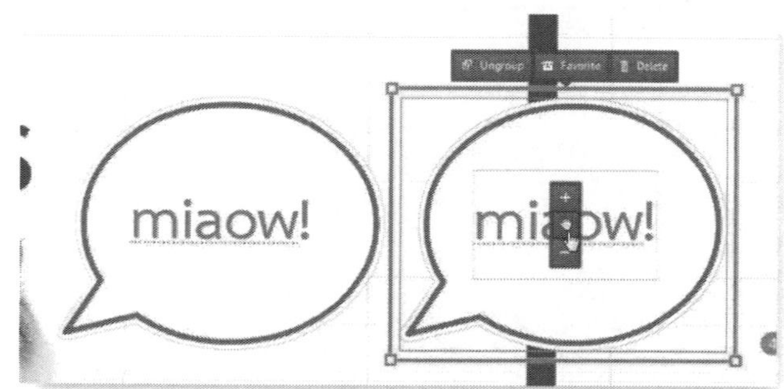

Ungroup the text and the bubble in the duplicated object and edit the text to a woof. Then group the two objects once more and drag this speech bubble into the Dogs frame.

STEP 10

Your canvas should look roughly like this. For maximum effect, what we need to do now is make the speech bubbles appear *after* the prezi has zoomed in on the Cats and Dogs frames. To do this, click the animation star in path point #2, the Cats frame. This frame will open in the animation window.

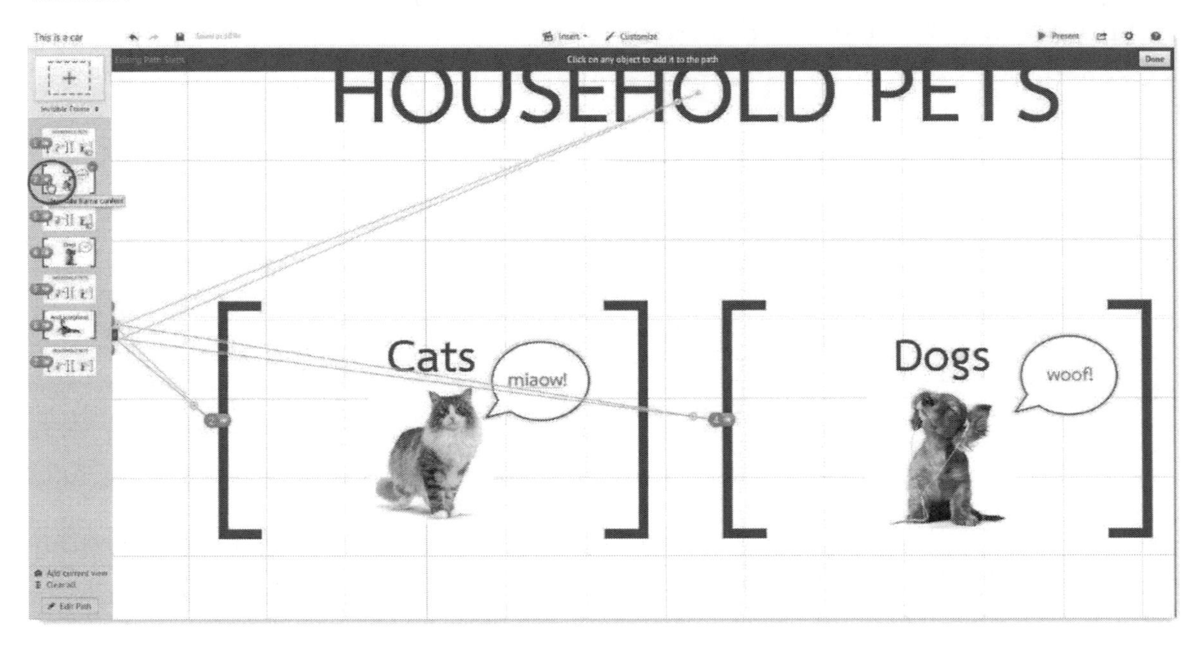

STEP 11

In the animation window, click the grouped bubble/text to apply the fade-in effect, and click **Done**. Repeat this for path point #4, the Dogs frame. If you like, make your Scorpion speak, too.

STEP 12

Now click Present and run through your prezi from start to finish. Here it is in full.

Feel free to grab a copy of my version here and deconstruct it:

http://bit.ly/prezi-pets

11 WORKING WITH VIDEO

If you've ever tried to get videos to play in PowerPoint, you know the deep, dark heart of terminal frustration. With Prezi, working with video is a breeze.

There are two ways to add videos in Prezi: insert a video file from your computer, or play one from YouTube. Just to be crystal clear about one thing: a YouTube video will *only* play if there is an internet connection during your presentation. The video isn't actually copied into your prezi; rather, it's just a link to the source video, much like embedding a YouTube video in a website. If you have no internet connection, or if the source video is removed on YouTube, it won't work in your prezi.

Given that you'd be madder than a box of frogs to rely upon a solid internet connection when you're speaking at a conference, we strongly suggest that you insert videos as files. This means that the video is saved within the prezi itself, just like an image or any other object. It will play regardless of internet connectivity.

There are plenty of tools that allow you to download videos from YouTube, such as the Firefox extension DownloadHelper: *www.downloadhelper.net*

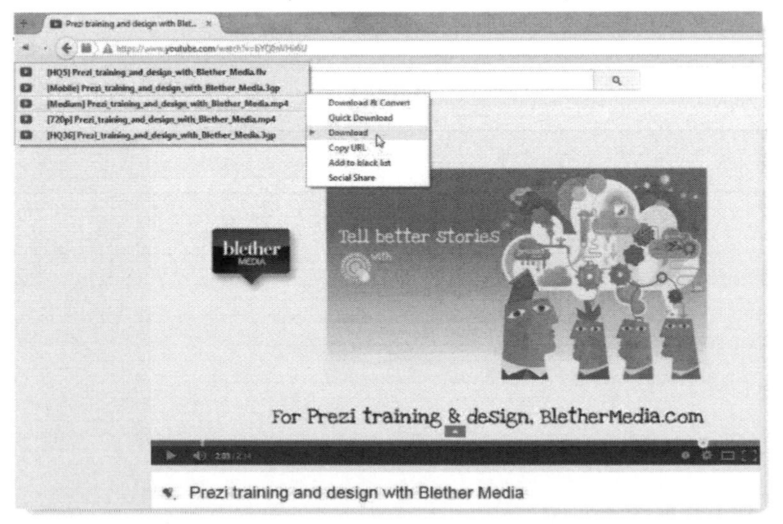

Be sure to respect the content owner's copyright when using YouTube videos (or any other content you find on the web). Wherever possible, use your own videos.

Prezi supports a bunch of video file formats, including FLV, F4V, MOV, WMV, F4V, MPG, MPEG, MP4, M4V and 3GP.

I have a particular preference for how I use videos in Prezi. This came about because I *always* forget when a video is about to play and find that I'm still talking when it starts. So I've adopted a five-click affair, and it goes like this:

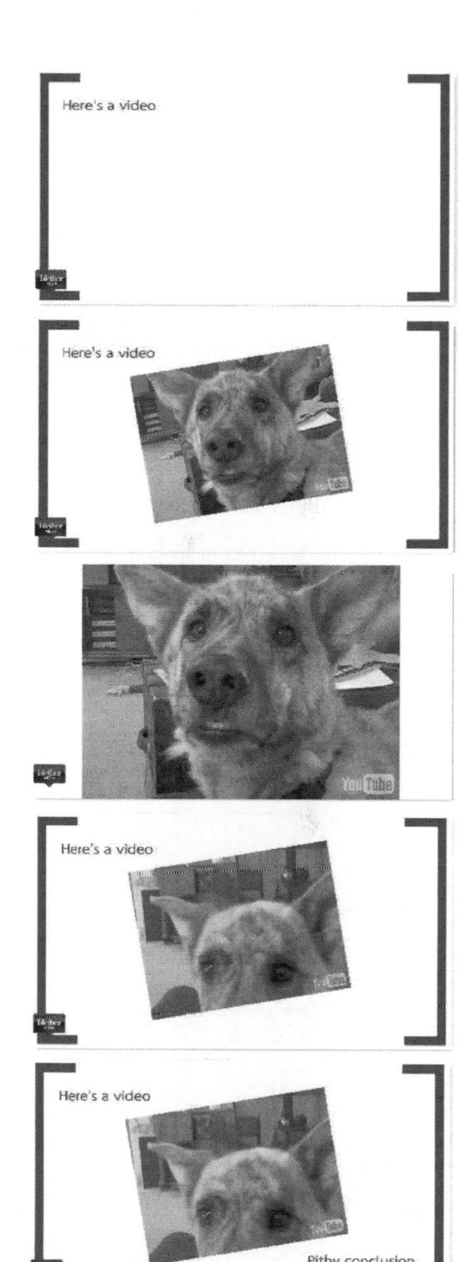

1. First, I flag that I'm going to introduce a video with an overview frame. The title would be relevant to the subject, obviously.

2. Next, I fade in the video on the canvas, which introduces a still-frame thumbnail. This will probably give the audience a clue about what they're going to see. I know that the next click will start the video playing so this is where I say a few words to introduce it.

3. When you make a video a path point, Prezi automatically plays it when you reach that point in the path. Just like any other path point, the video is displayed full screen.

4. As soon as the video is finished, another click takes me back to the overview frame and the thumbnail. If appropriate, I can discuss what we've just seen.

5. Finally, I like to end with a caption that summarises what we just saw, and why. This is the takeaway that I want the audience to remember.

You may prefer a different approach, of course, but let's quickly run through the process for doing it my way. There's nothing here that we haven't already covered: frame, path, and fade-in animation.

STEP 1

First, put a frame on the canvas – bracket, rectangle or invisible rather than a circle – and add a title and conclusion. From the Insert menu, either use the **From file** option to upload a video file or select the **YouTube video** option.

STEP 2

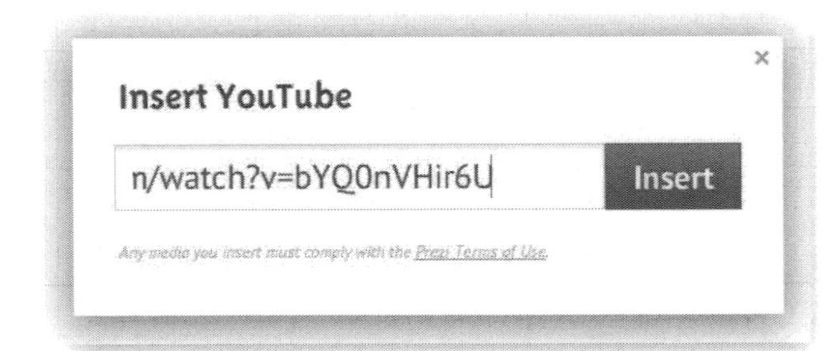

If you're using YouTube, first find the video on YouTube in your web browser and copy the full URL (web address). Paste the URL when prompted and click **Insert**.

STEP 3

The video will now appear on your canvas. Drag it into the right position in your overview frame between the title and the caption. Place it at a jaunty angle if you wish.

Now think about how many path points you need to achieve the sequence shown on p61. The answer is, of course, three – plus two fade-in animations.

STEP 4

Click Edit Path to open the path and add three path points.

- Path point #1 – the overview frame
- Path point #2 – the video
- Path point #3 – back to the overview frame

These path points correspond to steps 1, 3 and 5 on p61.

STEP 5

Now you need to apply fade-in animation to the video. Click the animation star for path point #1 to open the Animation window, and select the video. Click Done to close the window.

In path point #3, open the Animation window and select your pithy conclusion as the fade-in object.

That's all there is to it! You can use this approach to play videos at any point within your prezis. Have a look at my example here:

http://bit.ly/video-frame

12 WORKING WITH AUDIO

Prezi allows you to use sound files in two ways. First, you can add a background track that runs throughout a presentation. Secondly, you can add sound clips to individual path points. In that case, the clip plays when you reach the path point during the presentation.

For example, if you have a recording of your chief exec saying something particularly adroit, you could add their photo to the presentation, make it a path point, and add the recording as a sound clip that plays while the photo is on screen.

Prezi supports MP3, M4A, FLAC, WMA, WAV, OGG, AAC and MP4 files.

STEP 1

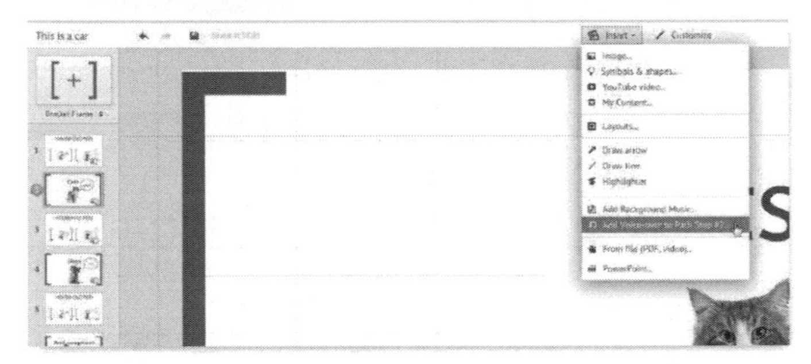

To add an audio clip to a path point, select the relevant path point in the **Edit Path** sidebar. Here it's path point #2. Now select the voice-over option from the **Insert** menu and upload your sound file.

STEP 2

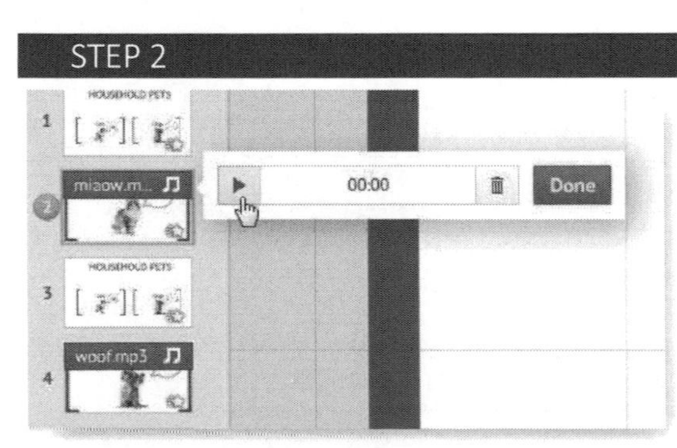

You can preview the effect in the **Edit Path** sidebar, or else just switch to **Present** mode and play your prezi. The sound file will play for as long as you remain on the path point. If you click to the next point in the path before the audio has finished, it will stop playing.

STEP 3

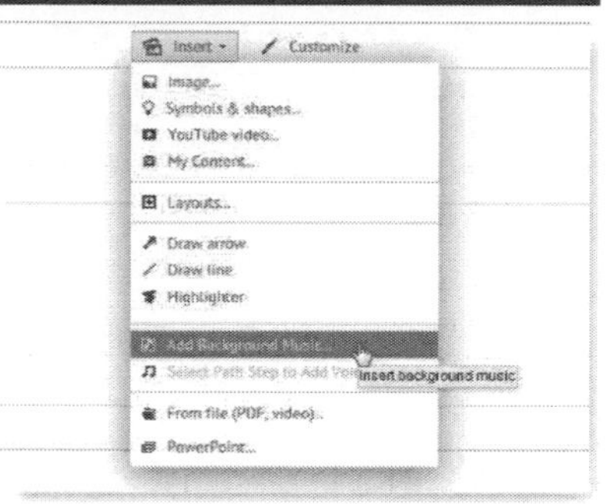

To add background music, click, er, **Add Background Music** from the **Insert** menu. Whatever audio file you upload here will play throughout your presentation. If the file finishes before the presentation is over, it just loops and starts again. If you have added any voice-over clips to path points, the background music will stop to allow that clip to play, and then continue when you click through to the next path point.

Background music is not really suitable when you're presenting live – it's likely to be a distraction – but it can work well if you're autoplaying a prezi in a loop on a display stand (see Step 5 on p80).

STEP 4

A caveat. Remember back on p57-58 where we faded-in a speech bubble to make the cat 'speak'? You might want to play some miaow-tastic audio just as this bubble appears, right? In fact, you can't. The bubble/text object was introduced to the canvas via fade-in animation *within* a path point. Audio clips can only be applied to actual path points.

A workaround would be to add an extra path point after the bubble/text appears. For instance, you could add an invisible frame like this and zoom in on the cat and its speech bubble. As the new frame fills the screen, the audio would play.

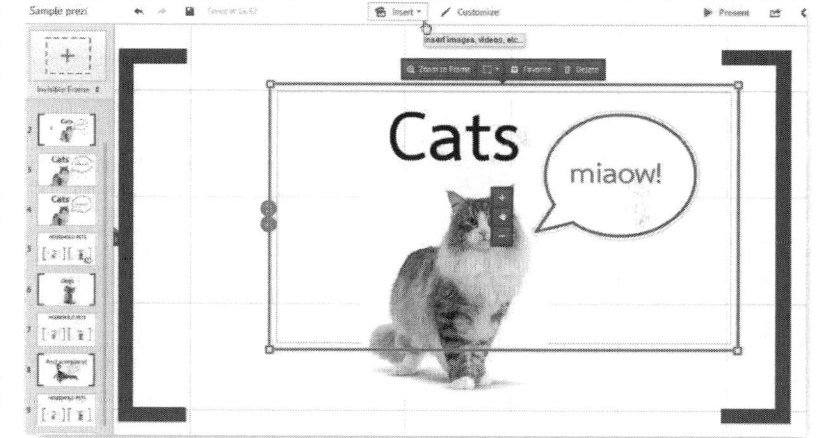

This limitation is just something to be aware of when designing your prezis.

13 (NOT) WORKING WITH POWERPOINT

One of the barriers to adoption for Prezi in the workplace is the prospect of having to recreate lots of old PowerPoints. Who has the time for that, no matter how funky Prezi is? It's often easier to stick with the status quo.

Not a bit of it! says Prezi. Simply import your PowerPoints directly into Prezi. Each slide becomes a frame and can be manipulated on the Prezi canvas just like any other object. You can even edit your slides. At a stroke, the barrier disappears. Convert your PPTs to Prezi!

That's the theory. In practice, Prezi's PowerPoint tool just doesn't work and I'm reluctant to spend any time at all on it. However, very briefly...

STEP 1

In any prezi, click **Insert** on the toolbar, and then **PowerPoint**. Select a PPT or PPTX file on your computer and wait while Prezi for Windows uploads and converts it.

STEP 2

Eventually, your converted PowerPoint should appear in a sidebar. You now have the option of inserting some or all of the slides on the prezi canvas. You can even choose a pretty pattern with a path built in. The idea, just to repeat, is that every slide becomes a frame and the content is editable.

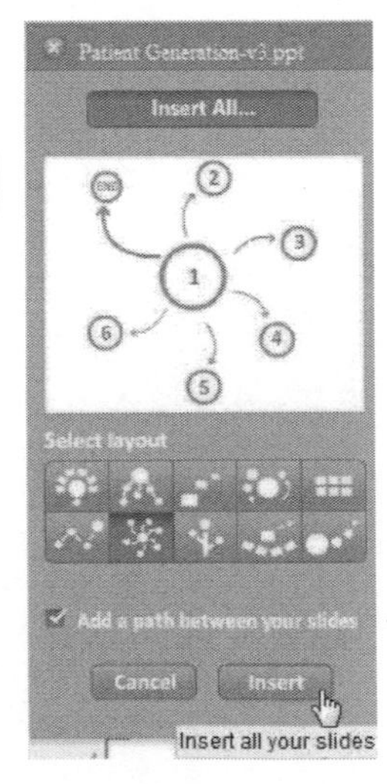

STEP 3

The reality is that your slides' layout and format will probably be messed up to the point of uselessness. I've very rarely seen a PPT import successfully – and if your PPT has any effects, forget it.

There is a workaround of sorts, which is to convert the PowerPoint file to a PDF file, and insert on the prezi canvas that way (via the **Insert** menu). There are some disadvantages – the content is no longer editable and you don't get the fancy layout options offered by a PowerPoint import – but overall it does tend to preserve the appearance of the original slides.

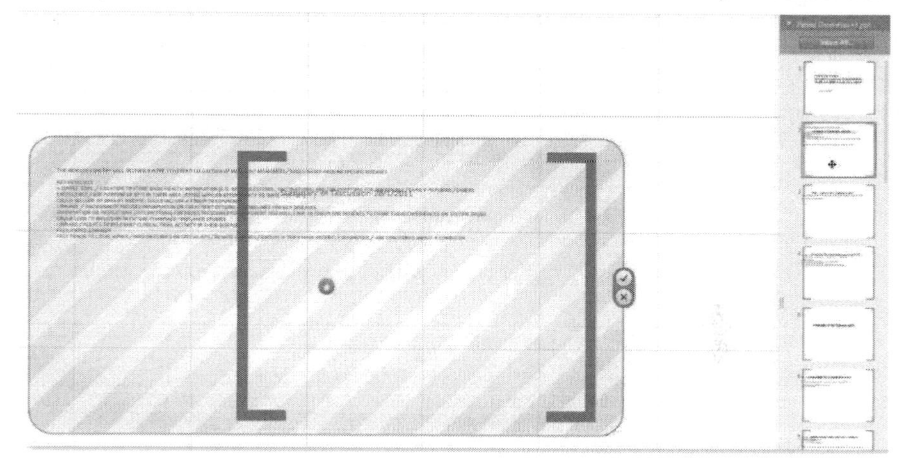

The question to ask yourself is why you'd want to preserve the look and feel of a PowerPoint presentation anyway? Isn't it better to start afresh in Prezi?

14 FAVORITES

In complete contrast to PowerPoint import, here's a super-useful feature! Whenever you think that you might want to reuse some content in a later prezi, add it to your Favorites. It couldn't be simpler...

STEP 1

When you have an object selected on the canvas, you'll see a Favorite button in the toolbar. Click this and a copy of the object will be saved to your Prezi account. You can do this with images, videos, frames full of content, and virtually anything else that's on the canvas.

STEP 2

Thereafter, whether you're working in Prezi for Windows or online, you can access saved content from the **Insert** menu. Select **My Content** and look in the Favorites section of the sidebar.

15 BACKGROUNDS AND TEMPLATES

So far, we've been working on a plain canvas. However, you can use an image as a prezi background and place content all over it. This can be a very effective way of telling a story, a bit like following a trail on a map.

You can also go further and create a pseudo 3D effect with a 3D background. Rather than placing content precisely on a fixed image, your prezi content 'floats' above a fluid background. This can also be very effective but the price you pay is a loss of positioning control. With a 2D background, you can position objects precisely on the image; with a 3D background, the background image is not static and you can never be quite sure where your foreground content will end up relative to it. If you use *three* 3D backgrounds, everything goes a little crazy. Still, crazy can be cool. Let's dive in.

STEP 1

To use an image as a fixed 2D background, simply insert it like any other image on the canvas and make it really big. You can then position frames and objects in layers on top of that image.

Consider using invisible frames in order not to detract from the background with the clutter of bracket, rectangle and circle frames.

STEP 2

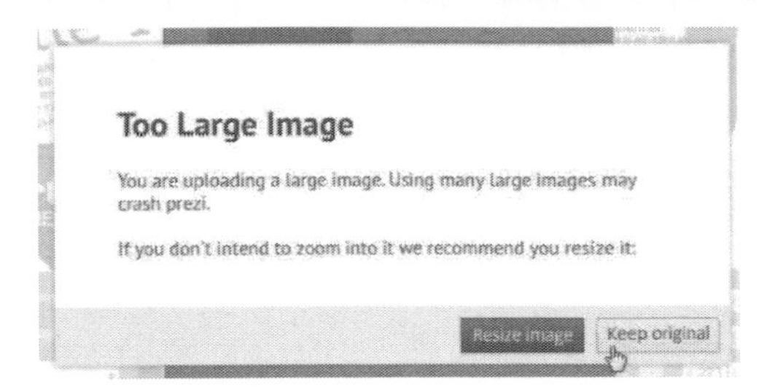

The main trouble with background images is the risk of pixilation (see p25), so either use high-resolution raster images, or vector images that scale without pixelation. This is when investing in quality photographs or diagrams from the likes of Shutterstock.com can pay dividends. Prezi will probably throw up a warning about file size but ignore this if you're inserting a background image. If you see this message when you're uploading an image for anything *other* than the background, take the resize option.

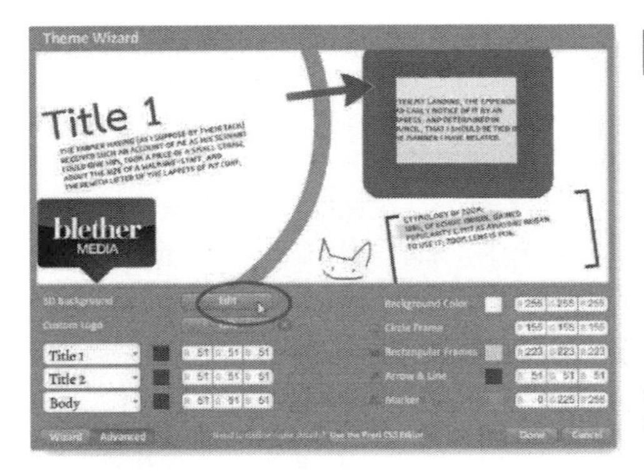

STEP 3

To experiment with 3D backgrounds, return to the Theme Wizard. Click **Edit** next to **3D Background**, select an appropriate image on your computer – there's no way to pull images from the internet here – and upload it.

STEP 4

Voila! When you present, your frames and other content will float above a fluid background, creating a 3D effect.

STEP 5

It's all very clever. It's can also be troublesome. In Step 4, I had to change the text colour to make my titles stand out against the strong background. The cat and dog pictures now look blocky and amateurish compared to when they sat against a plain white background. The background image is also pretty intrusive.

So, two tips. First, in the 3D context, a washed-out greyscale background is usually more effective than a full-colour image. You want to enhance the overall experience, not take attention away from your story. This version looks better, I think.

STEP 6

Secondly, images with transparency work well against both 2D and 3D backgrounds. Here, the white background has been removed from the dog on the right. It makes quite a difference.

STEP 7

Unlike 2D backgrounds, you don't – indeed, you can't – zoom in on a 3D background image, so pixelation is less of a concern. Neither is it an object on the canvas, so you can't select or manipulate it. A 3D background image is just sort of... there, and everything else happens in front of it.

Once you've uploaded a 3D background image, a thumbnail appears at the top of the **Customize** sidebar. You can delete it from here or try alternative images.

STEP 8

Back in Theme Wizard, visit the **Advanced** tab and click **Edit** next to **3D Background**. You can now upload three separate images as layers.

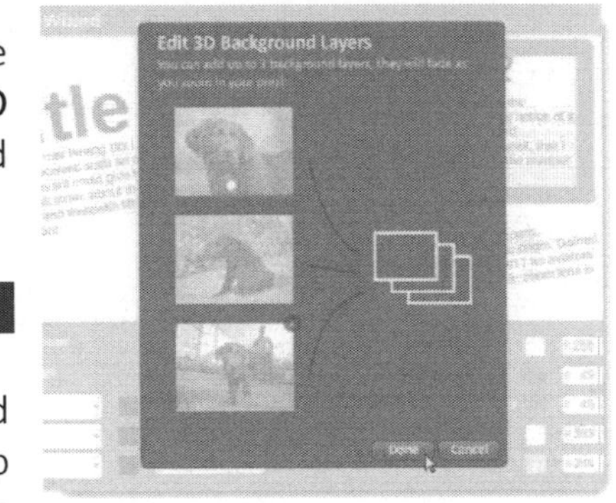

STEP 9

As you increase the degree of zoom on the canvas, the second 3D background image fades through and replaces the top image. Zoom some more and the third background fades through the second image. Zoom back out and you're back with the first background.

In this example, I have three 3D backgrounds and three circle frames on the canvas, nested within one another (you can't actually see frame #3 in the first image because it's relatively tiny). When frame #1 is made a path point and the prezi is presented, the top 3D background is visible. When I zoom to frame #2, the top background fades out and the second background fades through. Zoom again to frame #3 and we see the third background. Have a look at it here:

http://bit.ly/3d-zoom

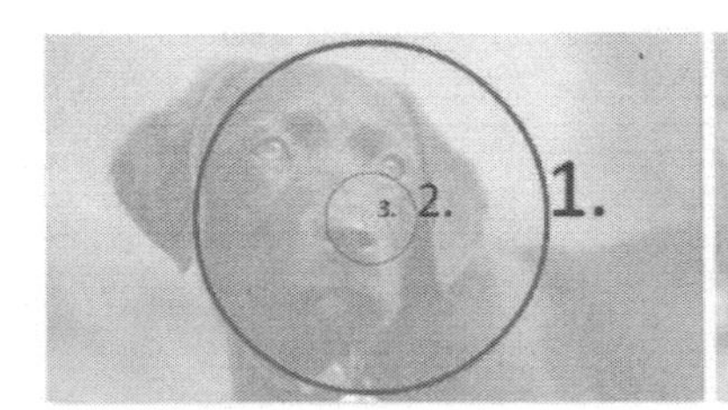

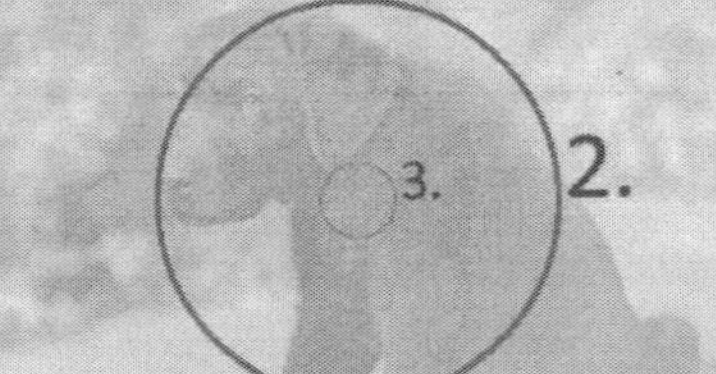

Now it's *very* much trial and error finding the right size for these frames to get them to work with the three backgrounds. However, if you have the patience to experiment, it can add a lovely effect to your prezis.

STEP 10

Prezi comes with a collection of ready-made templates, including a few that have 3D backgrounds. Most have 2D vector backgrounds that don't pixelate. Every time you start a new prezi, you have the opportunity to choose a template. Personally, I steer clear of templates because so many other people use them and prezis can end up looking pretty generic. That, and the fact that many Prezi templates are really cheesy. But if you need a shortcut, or just some inspiration, check them out.

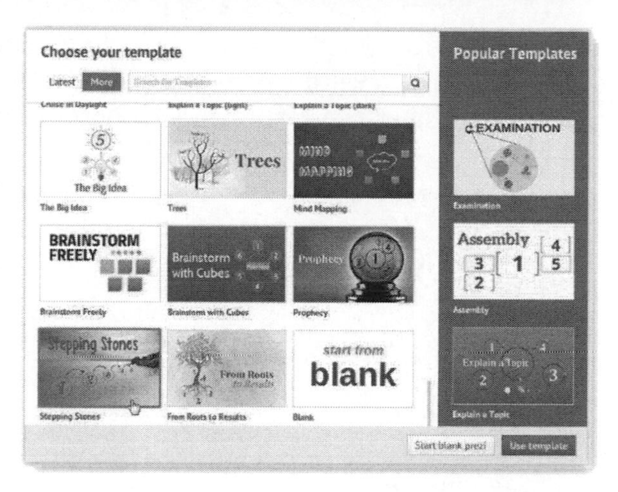

STEP 11

An alternative is to search on prezi.com for 'reusable' prezis. These are prezi designs that other Prezi users are happy for you to use. Search for keywords and check the **Show Reusable prezis only** box. Click on thumbnails to play prezis. Chances are you'll find something that you can use as the starting point for your own project.

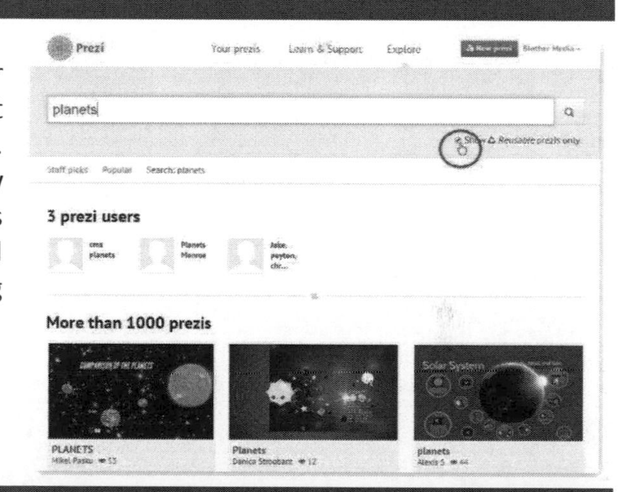

STEP 12

When you do see something you like, click the **Make a copy** button. A copy of the prezi will appear instantly in the **Your prezis** area of your own account on prezi.com. It's yours to do with as you please.

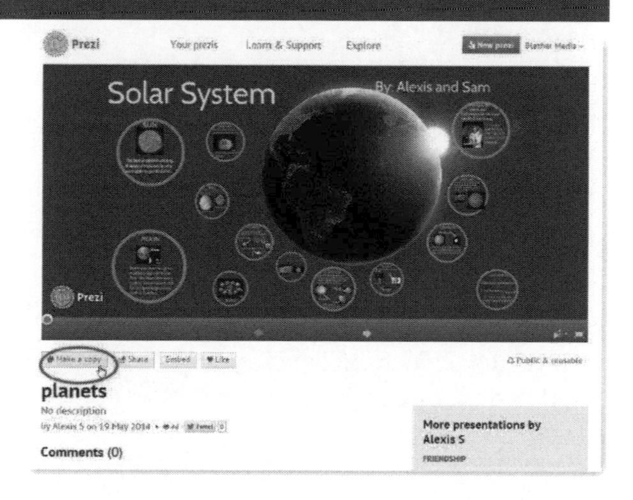

STEP 13

To get a resuable prezi onto your computer for editing in the desktop application, open Prezi for Windows and click **Refresh** in the **All synced prezis** section. Your new prezi will appear as a greyed-out thumbnail. Click this thumbnail to download the prezi. Now you can open and edit it in Prezi for Windows.

STEP 14

Top tip! Make a copy of the prezi before you do anything. That way, you'll always have the original to return to should you goof things up and need to start again. In fact, always make a copy of every prezi.

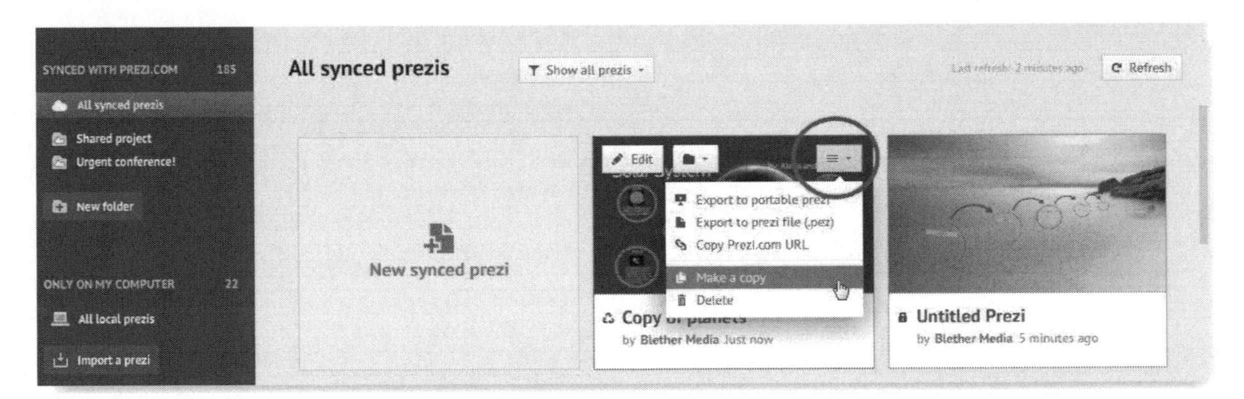

16 SHARING AND COLLABORATING

There will be times when you want to show somebody else a prezi to get their input, either indirectly in the form of feedback or directly in the form of collaboration. Because Prezi is an online cloud-based service, all of this is easy. In this section, we'll have to work on the prezi.com website rather than using Prezi for Windows.

STEP 1

Log into your account on prezi.com, open the **Your prezis** section, and click on any prezi. You can play the prezi on this page but for now note the row of buttons below the player window.

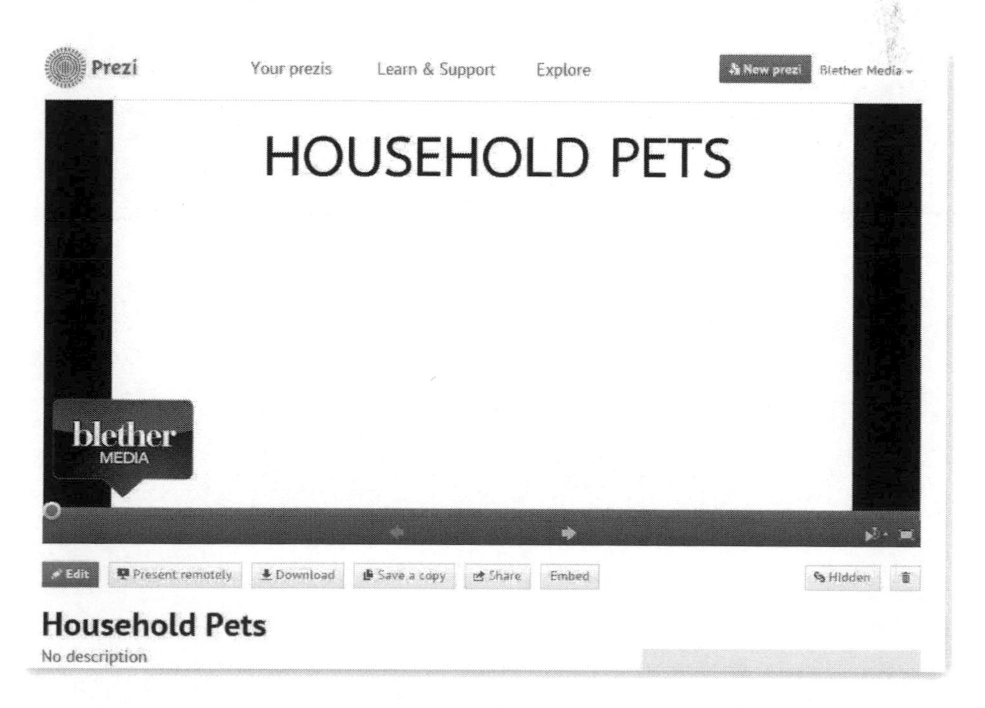

STEP 2

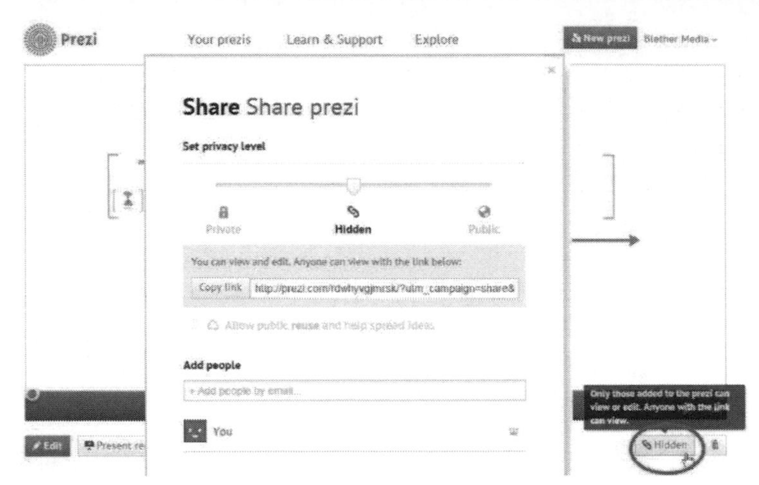

Click the privacy button in the bottom-right corner. In terms of who can see any given prezi, you can select between:

- Private – nobody but you
- Hidden – anyone with whom you share the link
- Public – anyone at all

All prezis created with an Enjoy or Pro account are hidden by default. The free version of prezi doesn't let you make prezis private so anything you create online can be seen by anyone who stumbles upon it. Note that you can *only* create prezis online with a free account; you don't get Prezi for Windows.

If you choose to make a prezi public, you can also check the reusable box to allow people to make their own copies, just as we did with a planet prezi in the previous chapter. Generally, though, the hidden option is ideal, as it keeps your prezi private while simultaneously allowing you to selectively share it.

STEP 3

When a prezi is hidden, you have some choices. Access these by clicking the **Share** button under the player window. You can copy the link and email it, in which case the recipient will be able to play the prezi in their own web browser. Alternatively, you can get Prezi to email them the link directly by entering an email address. In this scenario, you can also choose whether the recipient has the right to edit your prezi (select **Editor**). They'll need to have their own Prezi account for this, whereas anyone at all can be a viewer.

STEP 4

When you share an Editor link, the recipient can work on your prezi in their own time or at the same time as you. In fact, up to 10 people can collaborate in real time. You'll see live co-collaborators represented on the canvas by icons. You'll also find a sidebar on the right that shows who's currently logged in.

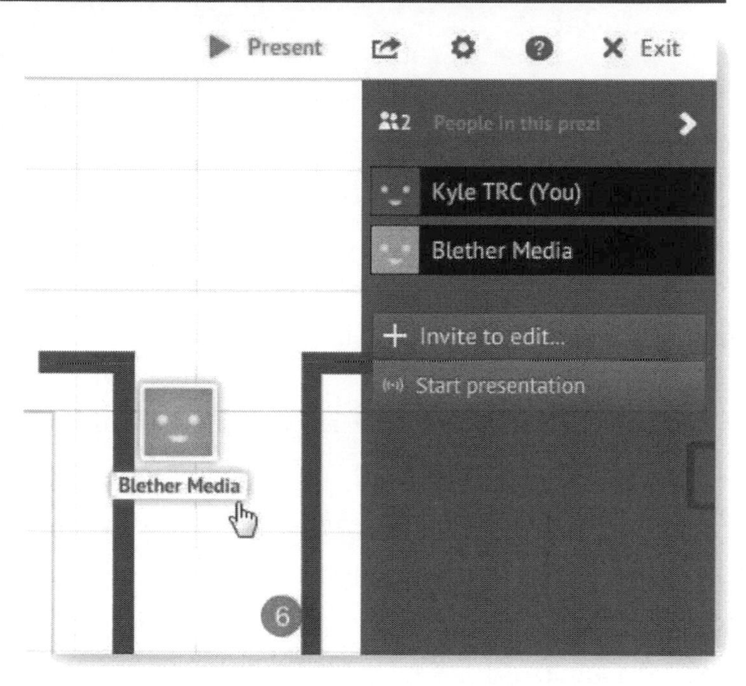

Note that people can work on different parts of the prezi at the same time, because each controls their own view of the canvas. Note too that it's perfectly possible to delete somebody else's work, so be careful!

Collaborating in real time can be useful. It can also be confusing, and you may prefer to take turns.

STEP 5

At any point, anyone who's collaborating can use the **Start presentation** button in the sidebar to switch to **Present** mode. Collaborators receive a notification which they can either accept in order to watch the presentation, or decline in order to carry on working.

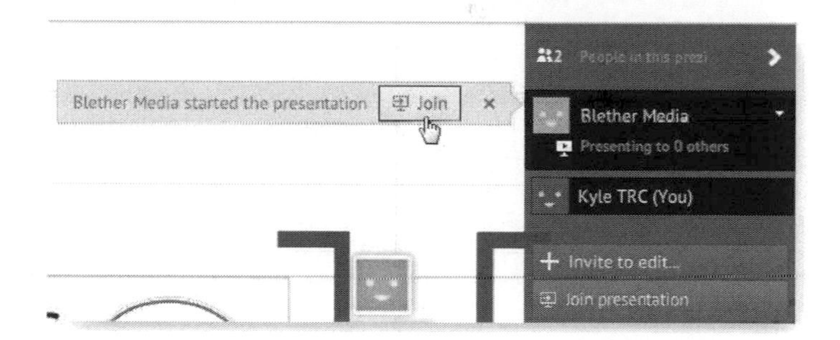

17 PRESENTING ONLINE AND OFFLINE

When it comes to presenting to an audience of one or a thousand, there are several ways to use Prezi. Which you choose depends upon whether:

- The audience is sat in front of you – or somewhere else entirely
- You're using your own computer in your own office – or unfamiliar equipment in a different location
- You have a guaranteed internet connection – or not
- You need to control the presentation – or you're happy for viewers to go through your story at their own speed
- You want your audience to watch a pre-programmed presentation with no involvement on their part or yours

There's some overlap here so let's just work through all the possibilities.

STEP 1

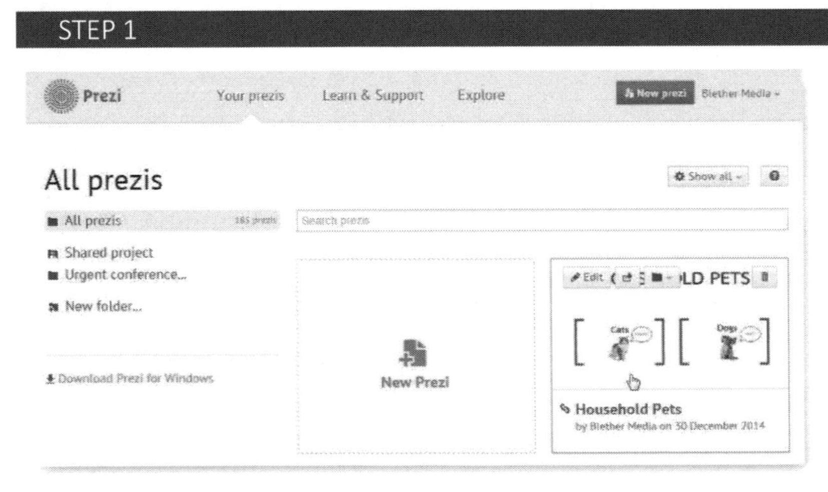

First, go to the **Your prezis** section in prezi.com and select any prezi that has a path. This will open it on the web page with the player window.

STEP 2

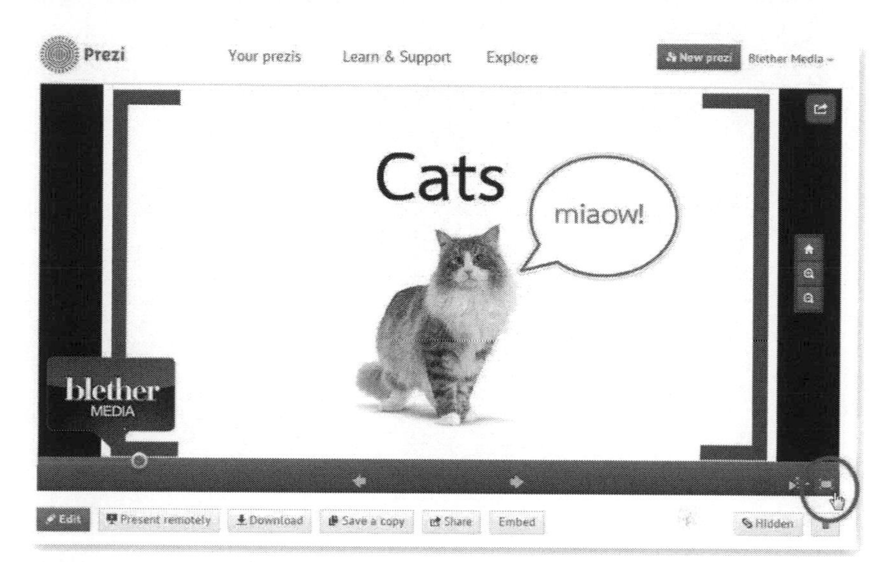

Use the left and right arrows to play your prezi. To go full-screen, click the button in the bottom-right corner.

You can present like this from any computer anywhere in the world (so long as it has an internet connection) simply by logging into your account on prezi.com. You can also, of course, connect the computer to a projector or display.

STEP 3

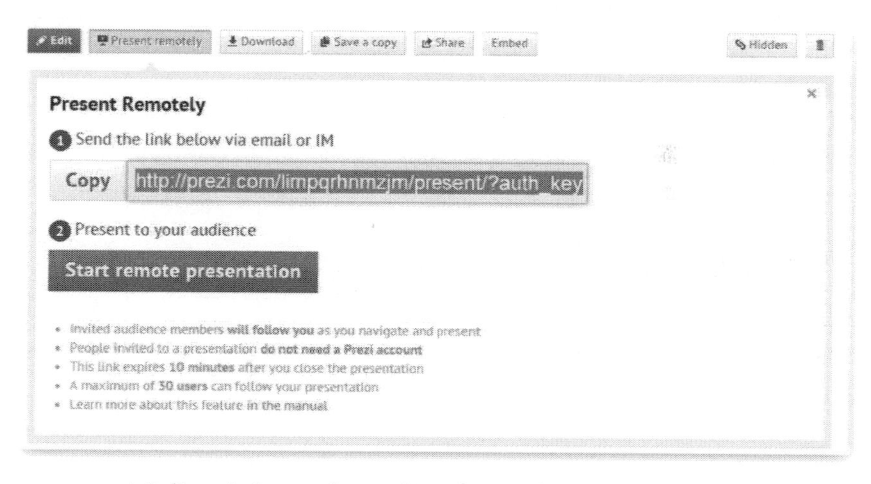

But what if your audience is somewhere else? One of Prezi's sweetest features is the **Present Remotely** option. Click this button – it's just under the player window – and you get a link which you can email to up to 30 participants. When they click the link, your prezi will open in their browsers and they can watch from anywhere as you present it live. It just takes a bit of coordination to get everyone clicking links and watching at the same time.

The major drawback is that they can't *hear* you so you'll probably need to set up a conference call or Skype session.

STEP 4

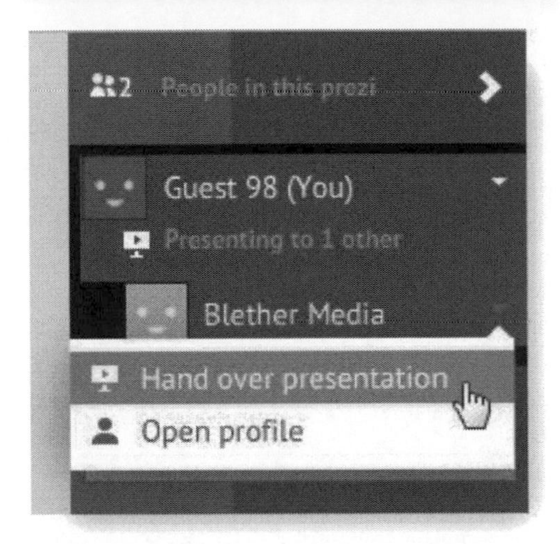

Note that you can hand over a remote presentation to any of the participants via the sidebar that we saw earlier (see Step 4 on p77). They then get to play the prezi while you watch.

This is a great feature that you'll just love when you're pitching remotely to a potential investor and they take over the reins to revisit and drill down into those financial projections that you skipped through earlier...

STEP 5

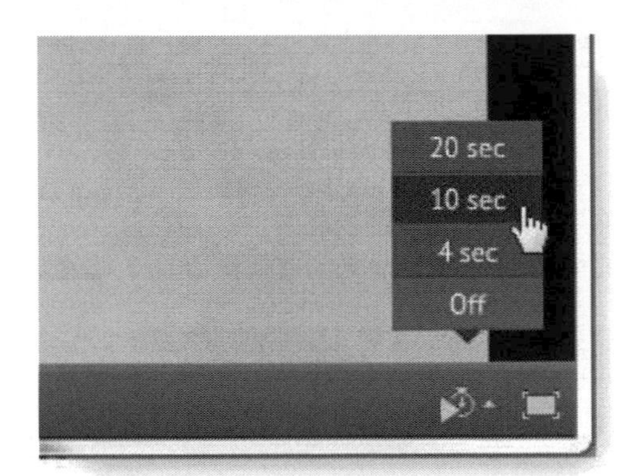

Let's suppose you have a stand at an exhibition with access to a display TV. You might play a video. But as you know, videos are expensive to make and really time-consuming to edit, render, produce etc. Why not use Prezi instead? A prezi can be displayed in full-screen mode and set to autoplay with 4, 10 or 20 second intervals between clicks. To see the options, click and hold the play button next to the full-screen button. Select **10 sec** and the prezi will play all by itself with 10 seconds between clicks. It will even loop when it's finished so you can happily leave it running all day. And of course you can easily edit it at any time.

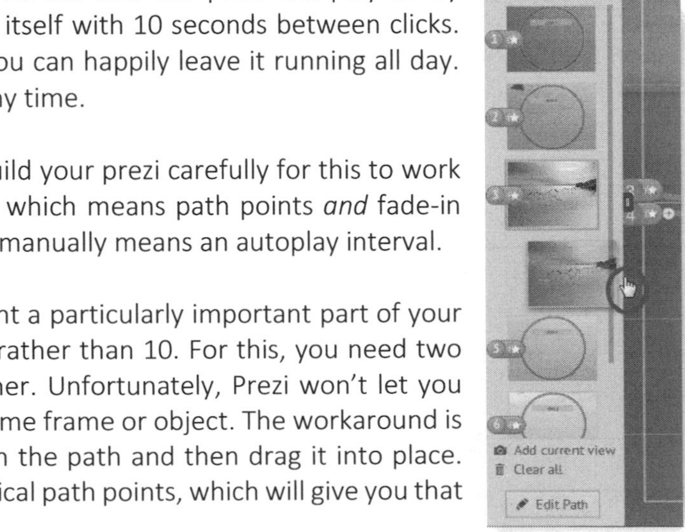

However, you do need to design and build your prezi carefully for this to work well. Autoplay intervals apply to clicks, which means path points *and* fade-in animations. Anything at requires a click manually means an autoplay interval.

Here's a tip for autoplay. You might want a particularly important part of your prezi to stay on screen for 20 seconds rather than 10. For this, you need two identical path points, one after the other. Unfortunately, Prezi won't let you make consecutive path points for the same frame or object. The workaround is to create the second path point *later* in the path and then drag it into place. This will give you two consecutive, identical path points, which will give you that 20-second interval.

STEP 6

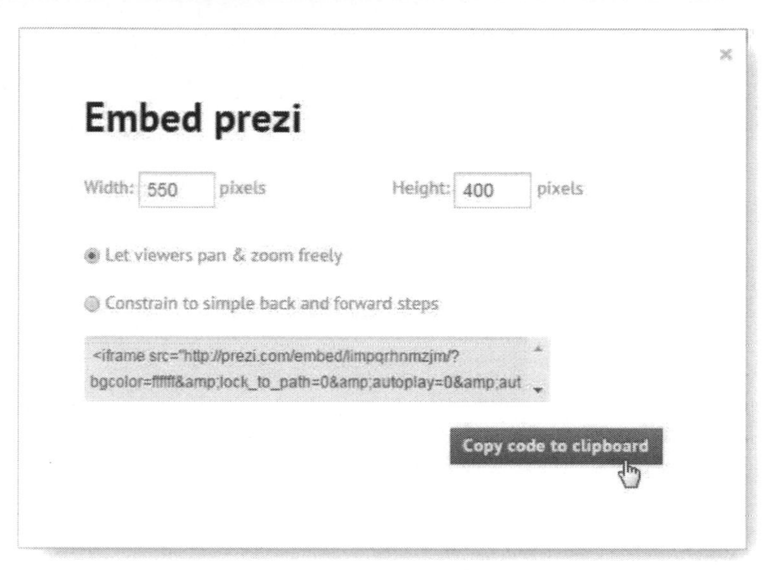

Another option for letting people see a prezi is to embed it on a website. This is very straightforward if you're familiar with web code: just click the **Embed** button under the prezi player, copy the code, and paste it into a web page.

There's an interesting choice to be made here, namely whether viewers can deviate from the path. If you allow them this freedom, they can follow the path *or* pan and zoom around the canvas at will. If your prezi is a visual map of some sort – perhaps a plan of a building – or if you're sharing with an audience of colleagues rather than strangers, this might be just what you need. But if you're trying to tell a coherent linear story, keeping viewers on the path will be safer.

It would be lovely, would it not, if you could embed a prezi and make it automatically start in autoplay mode, running from beginning to end a bit like a video? But you can't, sorry.

STEP 7

When I first started using Prezi, one of the revelations was that I could take my presentation with me anywhere on a USB stick and know, with absolute certainty, that it would play just fine regardless of what hardware or software I ended up using. Gone was all that uncertainty about creating a slide deck in PowerPoint 2007 and hoping it would work ok in PowerPoint 2003 if that's what the conference organiser happened to have (no, being the usual discovery).

Household Pets

Prezi does away with all of that angst with the 'portable' prezi. This is a self-contained version of a prezi presentation that includes its own player. It doesn't rely upon any software on the host computer and it works on PCs and Macs. It also, crucially, works without an internet connection. There's one downside, which is that a portable prezi is 'locked' and can't be edited, but that's a small price to pay for the security of being able to present offline anywhere, any time.

STEP 8

Because a portable prezi can't be edited, you would typically produce it only when you're entirely happy with your presentation. However, you can always return to your original prezi for re-editing, and you can make as many portable prezis as you like.

In prezi.com (see screenshot on the left), click the **Download** link under the player window and select the **Presenting** option.

Or if you're working in Prezi for Windows (see screenshot below), use the thumbnail menu to select **Export to portable prezi**.

In both cases, Prezi will create a Zip file. Download this file from prezi.com or save it from Prezi for Windows.

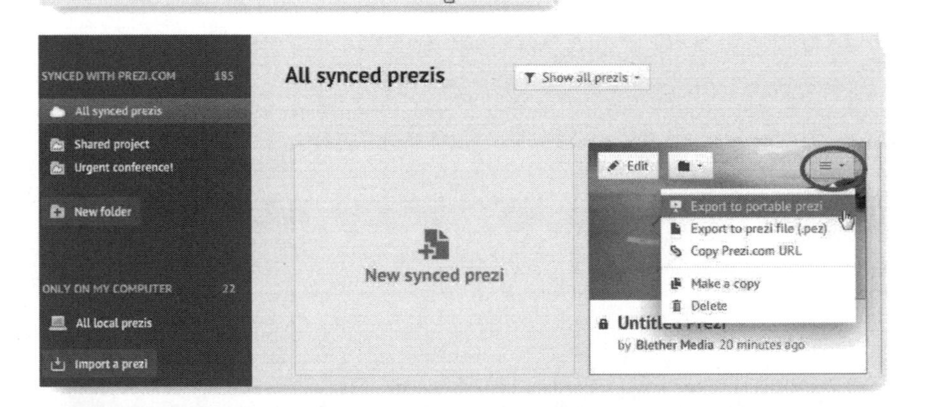

STEP 9

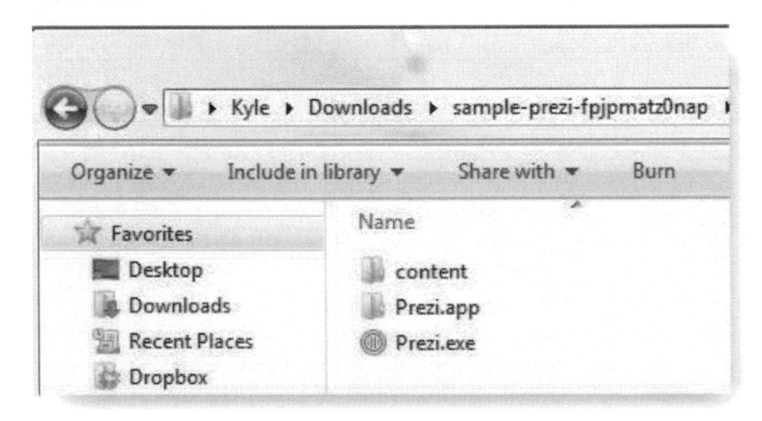

Now extract the Zip file on your computer to create a new, uncompressed folder.

Within this new folder, you'll find a folder called content, one called Prezi.app (this is for Macs) and a file called Prezi.exe. Double-click the Prezi.exe file to launch the portable prezi.

STEP 10

Huzzah! Your portable prezi will open in a self-contained player. You can use the arrows (or a presenter's clicker) to play it, and you can freely pan, zoom and explore, make it full-screen, and turn on autoplay. The one thing you can't do is make any changes.

Important notes:

- YouTube videos will work only if the computer you're using to present on has an internet connection. But embedded video files will work without the internet. That's always the safer option.
- It is essential to keep the folders and files seen in Step 9 together. So if you're copying your portable prezi to a USB stick, copy the top-level folder that you extracted from the Zip file. (If you just copy the Prezi.exe file, it won't work.)
- If you're emailing your prezi to someone, email the Zip file along with instructions on how to unzip it and play the prezi within.
- If you need to make changes to your prezi, make them in prezi.com or Prezi for Windows and download or export a fresh portable prezi.

18 ORGANISING YOUR PREZIS

As we have seen, you can syncs prezis between your computer and your Prezi account on the web. If you create a prezi in Prezi for Windows, you can upload a copy to prezi.com; and if you create a prezi on prezi.com, you can download a copy to Prezi for Windows.

But *should* you sync everything all the time? What's the best way to keep prezis in order? What's the best way to group multiple prezis in a project? And how can we share them?

STEP 1

Unfortunately, you only get 2 GB of storage with a Prezi Pro account, and that's really not a lot if you tend to embed hi-res video files in your projects. To avoid this limitation, I tend to create *local* prezis in Prezi for Windows and only sync finished prezis that I definitely want to keep (or share / collaborate on with clients). There's no restriction on how many local prezis you can have.

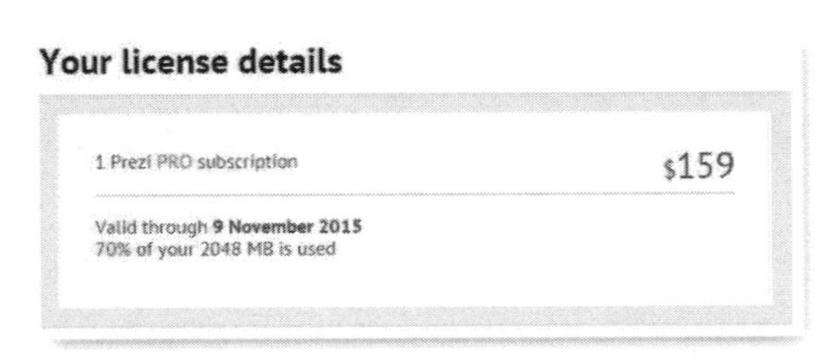

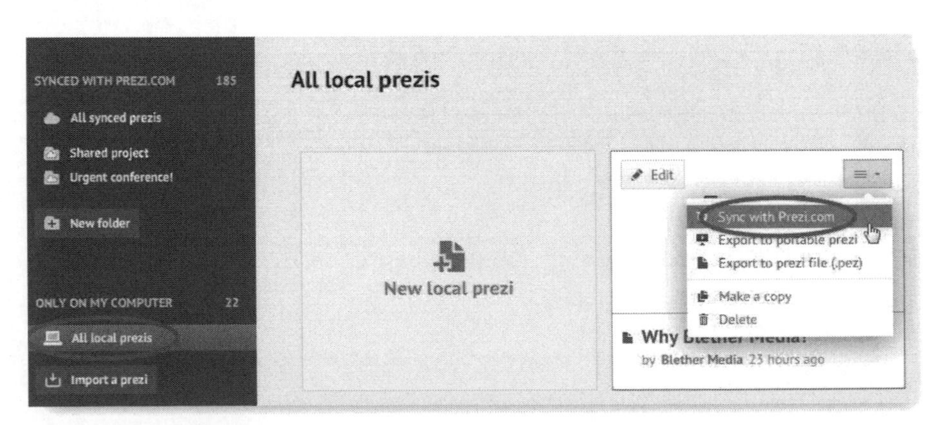

STEP 2

A relatively new but rather handy Prezi feature is that of folders. A folder is simply a way of filing prezis.

When you're in Prezi for Windows, click **New folder** in the **All synced prezis** section, and give it a name. Note that you can't file local prezis in local folders, which is a shame.

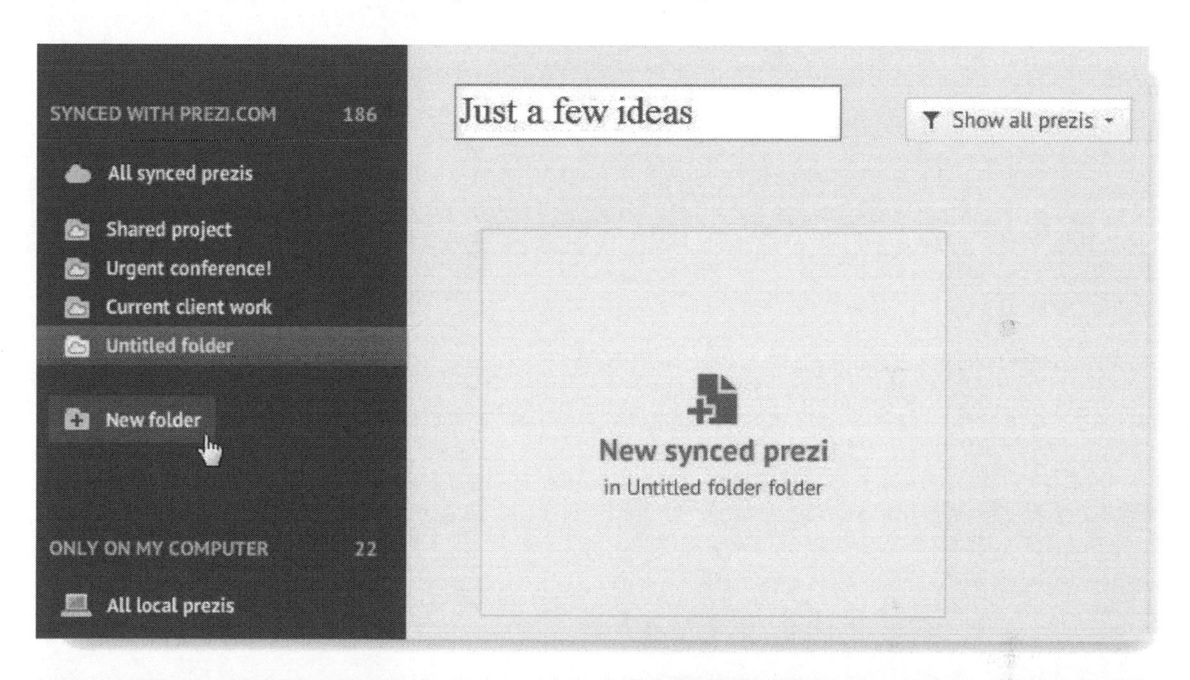

STEP 3

Move synced prezis into any folder via the thumbnail menu. Just check the appropriate folder name.

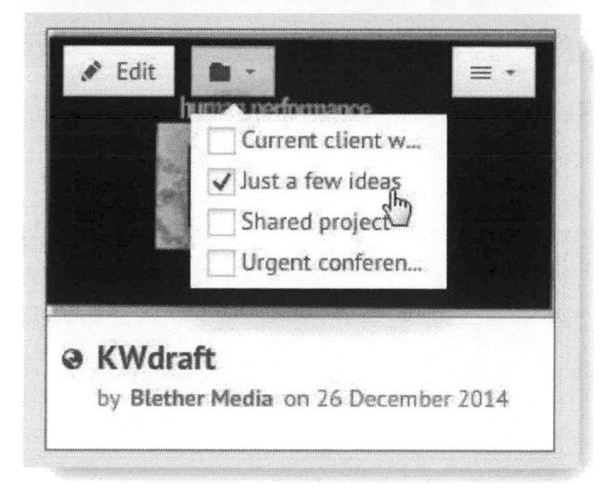

STEP 4

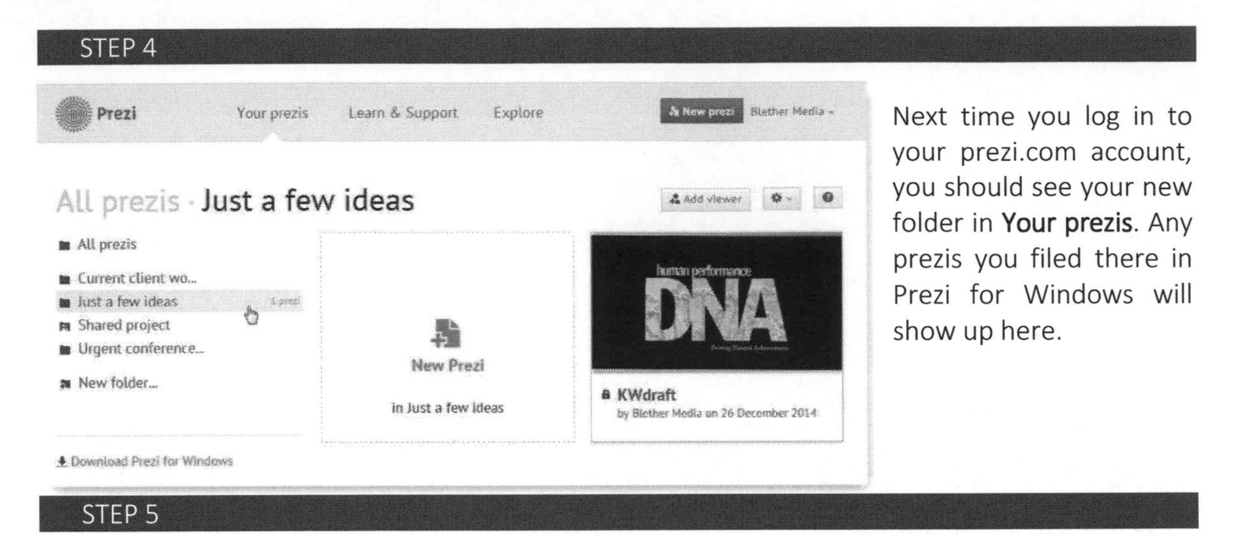

Next time you log in to your prezi.com account, you should see your new folder in **Your prezis**. Any prezis you filed there in Prezi for Windows will show up here.

STEP 5

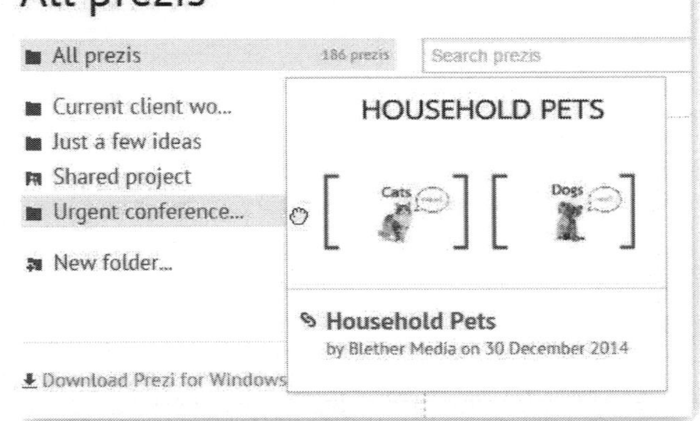

You can also drag and drop prezis from the **All prezis** section into any folder in the folder list. Here I'm dragging my household pets masterpiece into the **Urgent conference** folder. Anything you do in prezi.com will be reflected back in Prezi for Windows (though you may have to hit the Refresh button first).

STEP 6

To share a folder with others, you have to be in prezi.com rather than Prezi for Windows. Select a folder, click the cog icon, and click **Manage folder** from the menu.

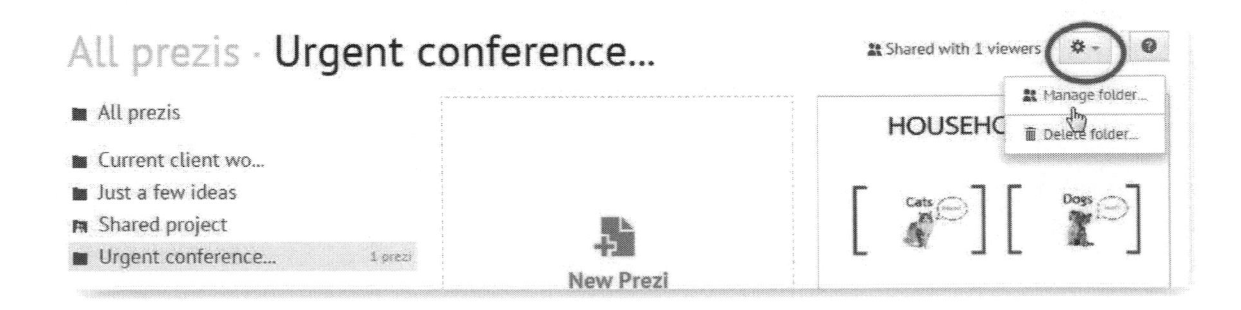

STEP 7

From the **Manage folder** menu, type an email address and hit **Add**. Repeat as necessary, and then click **Done**. Prezi will email your recipients with an invitation to share your folder. If they accept, they'll get a copy of the folder with its contents in their own Prezi accounts.

If you add a new prezi to a shared folder, it will automatically be shared with them.

STEP 8

By default, the people with whom you share a folder have only viewing rights. They can play the prezis in that folder but not edit them. However, you can control rights on a prezi-by-prezi basis using the **Share** options for each prezi.

Select a prezi and click the **Share** button below the player window. If the prezi is in a shared folder, you'll see a list of people who currently have access to it. Use the dropdown menu next to their names to make them viewers or editors. You can also kick people out of a folder here!

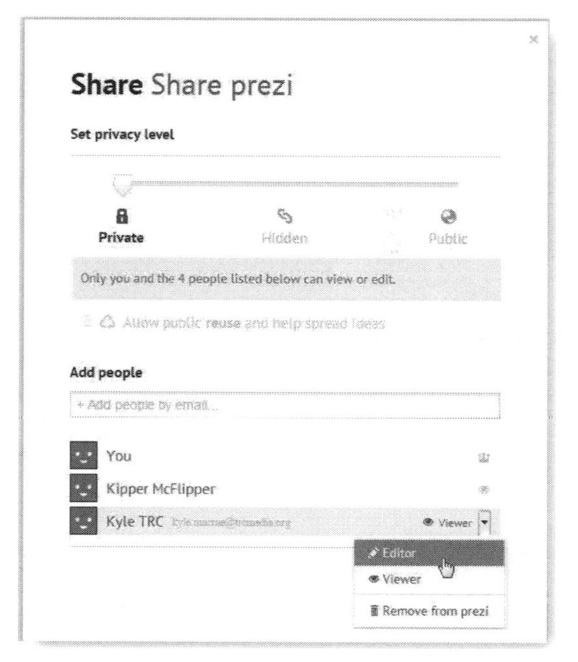

If you ever delete a folder (the option is in the **Manage Folder** menu), prezis in that folder are not deleted. They simply move back to your **All prezis** collection.

19 PRINTING HANDOUTS

How do you produce a printed handout from a prezi? Simple: open a prezi in Edit mode and click the Export button in the toolbar. If you're in Prezi for Windows, you can export and save a PDF. If you're in prezi.com, download and save it.

Ah, but how do you produce a *useful* printed handout? That's not so simple.

Prezi creates a page in the PDF for every path point. Let's say that you have an overview frame (path point #1) that contains two frames. Your presentation zooms into these frames (path points #2 and #3), and then back out to the overview (path point #4). Just like the Household Pets example in Step 12 on p49, in fact. Prezi will convert this to four pages in a PDF. This is neither great for the planet nor for your handout recipients. You would almost certainly want to print the overview frame as a single page, with no need to show the Cats and Dogs frames on separate pages.

The workaround is to print out the full PDF, throw away all the pages you don't want, and photocopy what's left...

No, not really. What you need to do is make a copy of the original prezi (see Step 12 on p73), clear the current path, and create a new path specifically for the handout. Remove all extraneous path points and fade-in animation effects and leave only those path points which you want to become pages. If necessary, add new frames / path points to change the layout of the prezi to suit a handout.

20 GOING MOBILE

Finally, just a word about Prezi's approach to mobile. As I write in early January 2015, the options are:

- Free iPad app – view, present, create and edit
- Free iPhone app – view and present only
- Android app – in the pipeline

There's something rather lovely about playing a prezi on an iPad, as the user experience is perfectly suited to pinch and zoom. Both the iPad and iPhone apps also allow you to present remotely, just as on p79. Creating a prezi from scratch on an iPad is a bit fiddly but as a backup to Prezi for Windows and prezi.com it's welcome indeed.

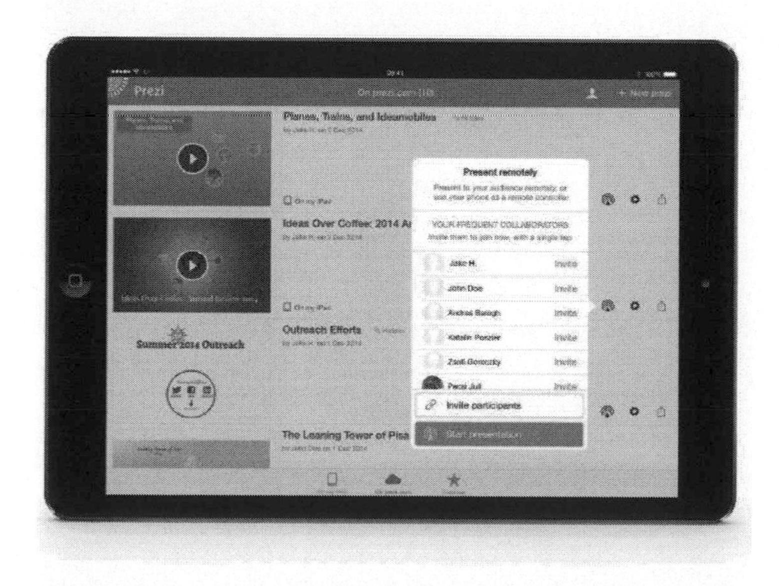

21 AND SO...

We're done! If you have followed this book step-by-step, page-by-page, you should now be in a position to create technically proficient prezis. So to wrap up, here's a challenge, an offer, a request and a pitch:

CHALLENGE Revisit the showcase prezis on prezi.com/explore and see if you can figure out how they have been made. Grab some reusable prezis and 'reverse engineer' them.

OFFER If you get stuck with anything, drop me an email and I'll do my very best to help. No charge. You can reach me at the email address below. If you'd like me to access one of your prezis, send a Viewer or Editor link to the same address (see Step 3 on p76).

REQUEST If this book has been useful to you, please take a moment to post a short review on Amazon. I'd really appreciate that!

PITCH We've been working at the technical level in this book. I know from my years of running Prezi training that most people get stuck or fed up at certain points, and I've hopefully addressed those here. You should now be a proficient prezi user. But the next challenge is *creative*. How do you take this technical knowledge and use it to design stunning, effective, memorable presentations?

Well, I'm working on a Prezi design book. If you would like to be notified when it's is available – and get an early-bird discount – sign up to my mailing list over at *www.blethermedia.com*

Oh, and if you'd like to commission me for a top-flight Prezi design or to deliver Prezi training to your company, that's cool too ☺

Cheers!
Kyle MacRae | kyle@blethermedia.com
January 2015, Glasgow

ABOUT THE AUTHOR

Kyle MacRae has a long history in consumer technology journalism and authored a dozen tech manuals for Haynes Publishing. He is also founder and managing director of Blether Media, which has specialised in Prezi training and design since 2009. He loves helping clients escape the constraints of PowerPoint!

www.blethermedia.com